The Open University

A207 FROM ENLIGHTENMENT
TO ROMANTICISM, c.1780–1830

# Block 2
# The Napoleonic Phenomenon

This publication forms part of an Open University course A207 *From Enlightenment to Romanticism, c.1780–1830.* Details of this and other Open University courses can be obtained from the Course Information and Advice Centre, PO Box 724, The Open University, Milton Keynes MK7 6ZS, United Kingdom: tel. +44 (0)1908 653231, e-mail general-enquiries@open.ac.uk

Alternatively, you may visit the Open University website at http://www.open.ac.uk where you can learn more about the wide range of courses and packs offered at all levels by The Open University.

To purchase a selection of Open University course materials visit the webshop at www.ouw.co.uk, or contact Open University Worldwide, Michael Young Building, Walton Hall, Milton Keynes MK7 6AA, United Kingdom for a brochure. tel. +44 (0)1908 858785; fax +44 (0)1908 858787; e-mail ouwenq@open.ac.uk

The Open University
Walton Hall, Milton Keynes
MK7 6AA

First published 2004. Reprinted 2005

Copyright © 2004 The Open University

Edited, designed and typeset by The Open University.

Printed and bound in Malta by Gutenberg Press.

ISBN 0 7492 8596 6

1.4

MIX
Paper from responsible sources
FSC
www.fsc.org  FSC® C022612

The paper used for this book is FSC-certified and totally chlorine-free. FSC (the Forest Stewardship Council) is an international network to promote responsible management of the world's forests.

# Contents

# Introduction to Block 2

*Prepared for the course team by Emma Barker and Antony Lentin*

History will decide: I am far from fearing it, I invoke it!

(Napoleon, 3 April 1816, in Las Cases, *Mémorial de Sainte Hélène*, 1983, p.489)

The popular sense of 'phenomenon' is 'a highly exceptional or unaccountable fact or occurrence' (*Shorter Oxford English Dictionary*). Napoleon Bonaparte was certainly that. A fellow Corsican and lifelong adversary, Pozzo di Borgo, described him as 'this phenomenon the like of whom shall never be seen again' (Schom, 1994, p.320). A second sense of 'phenomenon' is the outward appearance of things, and implies a contrast with the inner or underlying reality or truth. In this block we invite you to engage with 'the Napoleonic phenomenon' in both senses, and to respond to Napoleon's invocation of history which heads this introduction.

Among the many factors that made Napoleon a phenomenon in the first sense was, above all, the extent to which he was a self-made man. He rose from comparative obscurity to become the supreme ruler of a great continental empire and, in so doing, demonstrated how an individual of talent and merit could challenge the weight of tradition and authority. In this respect, he is a peculiarly modern figure. Napoleon's rise was not simply the result of his own exceptional abilities, however, but was made possible by the French Revolution, which had overthrown the Bourbon dynasty and left a power vacuum at the top. When Napoleon seized power in 1799, it was as the 'son of the Revolution', or more precisely as a general of the Revolution, committed to protecting both its internal gains and the frontiers of the republic, expanded and still expanding under his military leadership. At the same time, the imperial regime that he established can be seen as representing a reversion to the authoritarian traditions of the pre-revolutionary monarchy of the Old Regime. However, Napoleon could not simply turn the clock back and ignore the democratic legacy of the Revolution. Both as First Consul from 1799 and as emperor from 1804, his title derived theoretically from the sovereignty of the people and depended in practice on the support of public opinion. Throughout his rule he appealed to public opinion, occasionally through plebiscites but continuously through his direction of propaganda and the arts. 'Man', he reflected significantly, 'can only be governed through the imagination' (Fisher, 1971, p.147). As we will see in detail in Unit 9, which explores Napoleon's use of art as propaganda, he played a major role in shaping his own image from the time that he first came to public attention with a series of spectacular early victories, and he took care that the works of art he commissioned presented the Parisian audience who viewed them with a heavily edited version of 'reality'.

This brings us to Napoleon as a phenomenon in the second sense and to the peculiar difficulty of pinning down the man behind the myths. There are several reasons for this. The first is that much of the evidence about him, especially the evidence deliberately left by him – the written sources just as much as the painted images – is itself open to doubt and demands careful scrutiny. We need to consider his motives and intentions at the time in answering the question: how far can we rely on it? Second, Napoleon has proved uniquely controversial. No one is indifferent to him, and this has led to a variety of verdicts. Beginning with his contemporaries, the arguments for and against Napoleon have continued unabated. Conclusions are often passionately held but are not always easily reconcilable. It was like that in his own day, as you will see when you study the main text associated with Units 7–8: *A Life of Napoleon* (1817–18),[1] in which Stendhal takes up Napoleon's defence in vehement opposition to the hostile interpretation left by Mme de Staël in 1818 (part of which you will also consider). Finally, Napoleon himself, both as a man and as a ruler, seems to defy straightforward definition and interpretation. This is bound up with the fact that the values and ideals that he supported and represented were not stable but changed over time, as he moved from brilliant young republican general to authoritarian emperor. This also helps to explain why he has been so controversial; it was as a traitor to the original libertarian ideals of the French Revolution that Mme de Staël, an ardent champion of liberty, opposed him. All in all, to cite Pozzo di Borgo again, 'he is a great enigma and almost impossible to explain' (Schom, 1994, p.320).

One thing that can be said with confidence about Napoleon (and this is also part of the reason why a block of this course has been devoted to him) is that he is a transitional figure, one who straddles the boundaries between different political orders and different world views. Crucial to understanding this aspect of the Napoleonic phenomenon is the concept of 'genius'. Enlightenment thinkers were fascinated by the notion of genius, since it raised to the fore those exceptional persons whose outlook and activities, by definition, did not conform to the norm, to the rational, measured, closely defined lines of taste and conduct which lay at the heart of the Enlightenment mindset. The idea of genius prefigures some of the central concerns of Romanticism. 'Men of genius' were to be clearly distinguished from 'great men', the latter recognized as being more beneficial to society by virtue of their disciplined rationality, purposefulness and moderation in the cause of progress. 'Genius' was fascinating but troublesome, with its emphasis on the exceptional and the extraordinary, its tendency to break out into the irrational, the excessive and the self-destructive. Voltaire's *History of Charles XII* (1731) was about one such 'genius', the warrior-king of Sweden (r.1697–1718), whose legendary bravura culminated in his invasion of Russia in 1709, a

---

[1] References in this block to your edition of Stendhal, *A Life of Napoleon*, are abbreviated as LN.

venture ending in disaster and the subsequent ruin of his country. Samuel Johnson summed up Charles in his poem *The Vanity of Human Wishes* (1749):

> He left the name, at which the world grew pale
> To point a moral, or adorn a tale.

(lines 221–2)

By contrast in his *History of the Russian Empire under Peter the Great* (1760–3), Voltaire applauded the positive, creative, reforming achievement of Charles's adversary, Peter the Great (r.1696–1725), the 'great man' whose rational energy transformed Russia into a modern European state. And yet it was Johnson himself, the voice of reason *par excellence,* who appreciated the lure of pre-Romantic sensibility as against Enlightenment good sense, observing to Boswell in 1778:

> Were Socrates and Charles the Twelfth of Sweden both present in any company, and Socrates to say, 'Follow me, and hear a lecture in philosophy;' and Charles, laying his hand on his sword, to say, 'Follow me, and dethrone the Czar;' a man would be ashamed to follow Socrates.

(Boswell, 1951, p.191)

Napoleon famously exerted this pull over his followers. A century after Charles's defeat in Russia, he was at the height of his power, heading a continental empire with hegemony over 80 million Europeans and a multinational army of over half a million men. In 1812 he led this colossal force into Russia, following Charles's example with similar expectations and similar disastrous consequences – the destruction of his empire and his own downfall. Here might be seen the dangerous element of excess in what Stendhal called 'one of the greatest geniuses who ever lived' (LN, p.167) (though Stendhal himself argues that the invasion of Russia was rational and necessary). Unlike Charles, however, Napoleon had hitherto for a dozen years demonstrated an extraordinary flair for administration and legislation, somewhat in the manner of the 'enlightened absolutism' of the eighteenth century but on an incomparably greater scale. He introduced modern rules, regulations, procedures, institutions and reforms, notably the famous Civil Code or Code Napoléon, whose influence long outlasted him in France and several of the states under his control. His outlook as ruler and law-giver was inspired by Enlightenment rationalism and what he called *le beau idéal de la civilisation* (the splendid ideal of civilization). Goethe, an unswerving admirer, poetically evoked Napoleon's analytical and organizing vision, the radiant lucidity of mind that pared problems down to essentials and produced lasting solutions:

> What centuries have dimly meditated
> His mind surveys in brightest clarity.

(Quoted in Herold, 1955, p.xvii)

In Enlightenment terms, then, Napoleon partook both of the constructive qualities of the 'great man' and of its less predictable, more volatile counterpart, the 'man of genius'. The 'man of genius' is strongly marked by what Romantics would call the artistic temperament. As examples of the genius who transcends the sphere of great talent and excellence and is carried away into a category wholly out of the ordinary, Saint-Lambert in his article 'Genius' in the *Encyclopédie* cites the tragic actor performing a play by Corneille or Voltaire. And it is significant not only that Napoleon was a friend of the tragic actor Talma and was addicted to the tragedies of Corneille and Voltaire, but also that he consciously promoted his own 'image'. He was constantly concerned with appearances: the sweeping gesture, the grandiose scene, the moving declaration, the glory and nobility characteristic of French classical drama (and its models in Greece and Rome), which he, like his contemporaries, imbibed in his youth and sought to emulate on the world stage when he came to power.

The official dominance of Classicism (or Neoclassicism, as the classically-inspired art of this period is usually known) under Napoleon found expression in the 'empire style' of interior decoration, the Roman-style busts and statues of himself, the Vendôme column and Arc de Triomphe du Carrousel in Paris, the military bulletins and proclamations. At the same time, however, the fostering of a cult of personality in order to sustain Napoleon's hold on power encouraged a tendency in the propaganda art commissioned by the regime towards **painterly** effects, brutal violence and picturesque exoticism – all of which point the way towards the fully-fledged Romanticism of the 1820s. It is also possible to discern in the unofficial art of the Napoleonic era a shift towards a heightened concern with the irrational, with inner feelings and private suffering, all of which can be seen as characteristic of Romanticism as a broad cultural movement. Napoleon himself was not immune to these trends, as is clear from his enthusiasm for the 'rediscovered' poetry of the Scottish bard Ossian, published in 1760 (in fact concocted by James MacPherson: see Unit 1, p.35); two paintings on Ossianic themes decorated his country retreat, Malmaison. The one illustrated here sums up the melancholy mood of the poems; it shows the old, blind bard with his harp mourning the dead warriors and maidens whose ghosts populate the eerie, moonlit landscape. However, it is important to note that these paintings were private commissions. Classicism remained the official style of the regime, and a public championing of Nordic literature (of which Ossian was thought to be a typical example), such as Mme de Staël made in her important book *De l'Allemagne* (*On Germany*, 1810), implicitly challenged Napoleonic authority.[2] Napoleon had her book proscribed and pulped. In the German territories annexed to his empire he also took care to ban Schiller's pre-Romantic and Romantic tragedies,

---

[2] Mme de Staël was also initially a fan of Ossian, to whom she devoted a key role in her earlier work, *De la littérature* (1800). His omission from *De l'Allemagne* suggests that she had by then discovered that the work was a forgery.

*François Gérard,* Ossian Summoning the Spirits with the Sound of his Harp on the Banks of the Lora*, 1801–2, oil on canvas, 180.5 x 198.5 cm, Châteaux de Malmaison et Bois-Préau, Paris. Photo: © RMN/Arnaudet.*

*The Robbers, William Tell* and others – they were vehemently republican and libertarian.

Much of the following three units (and Audio 3, tracks 8–12) are devoted to *images* of Napoleon, both verbal and visual, laudatory and hostile. He is variously represented as a dashing military hero, agent of national salvation, vigilant civic administrator, saintly benefactor, laurel-wreathed monarch, classical tyrant, the incarnation of evil, and (according to Stendhal) too soft-hearted and trusting for his own good. The challenge of trying to make sense of this wealth of often contradictory images helps to explain his enduring fascination. The fact that his stereotype is still instantly recognizable (the bicorne hat, hand tucked in waistcoat, etc.) testifies both to the sheer success of his propaganda machine and to the enduring potency of the Napoleonic legend.

# References

Boswell, J. (1951) *The Life of Samuel Johnson*, London, Dent.

Fisher, H.A.L. (1971) *Napoleon*, London, Oxford University Press (first published 1912).

Herold, J.C. (ed.) (1955) *The Mind of Napoleon: A Selection from his Written and Spoken Words*, New York, Columbia University Press.

Las Cases, E. de (1983) *Mémorial de Sainte Hélène*, Paris, Flammarion.

Schom, A. (1994) *One Hundred Days: Napoleon's Road to Waterloo*, Harmondsworth, Penguin.

# Units 7–8
# Stendhal's *A Life of Napoleon* and other contemporary sources by or concerning Napoleon

*Prepared for the course team by Antony Lentin*

# Contents

# Study components

| Weeks of study | Supplementary material | Audio-visual | Anthologies and set books |
|---|---|---|---|
| 2 | AV Notes<br>Illustrations Book | Audio 3<br>Video 2 | Anthology I<br>Stendhal, *A Life of Napoleon* |

The required reading from *A Life of Napoleon* is as follows: preface, chapters 1, 3–4, 8, 11–13, 15–16, 18–25, 27, 30, 32–35, 40, 43–51, 54, 57–68, 72, 74–5, 77, 79, 82, 86–7.

You should aim to complete sections 1–5 of these units in the first week and sections 6–10 in the second week. In the course of these units you will be asked to focus on short extracts from the text, Stendhal's *A Life of Napoleon*, as part of some of the exercises. Otherwise, your reading of the book is not guided, and while we recommend that you aim to complete the required reading by the end of the first week, it is for you to choose your own time to do so. As you go through the book, you may find it helpful to make brief notes on, or highlight words or passages which strike you as noteworthy or revealing about, Stendhal's attitude to Napoleon. (The units make occasional references to passages outside the set reading, but you are not obliged to follow these up.)

# Objectives

By the end of your work on Units 7–8 you should:

- be aware of the main facts of Napoleon's career,[1] and be able to discuss and assess critically and in an informed way his character, rule, and historical and cultural significance in the period *c.*1800–30;

- through the critical examination of selected primary sources be aware of Napoleon's skill at self-presentation and appreciate the basic problems involved in evaluating evidence and establishing historical facts;

- appreciate the issue of subjectivity in historical interpretation and be able to form a view of the nature of Stendhal's *A Life of Napoleon* and its reliability;

- be able to test and compare Stendhal's presentation of Napoleon against other sources – in particular, the account by Germaine de Staël.

---

[1] Your edition of Stendhal's *Life of Napoleon* includes a chronology of Napoleon's career.

# 1   Introduction

The inclusion of a text on Napoleon Bonaparte (1769–1821) in a course entitled *From Enlightenment to Romanticism* needs no apology. That unique figure is central to the course. He gives his name to an epoch of European history from 1799 to 1815 – the Napoleonic era. He bestrides both Enlightenment and Romanticism, he is acknowledged as 'the supreme figure of the Romantic period' (Bainbridge, 1995, p.9), and his historical significance remains the subject of unending debate (see Geyl, 1965).

'From nothing,' Napoleon reflected, 'I raised myself to be the most powerful monarch in the world. Europe was at my feet' (Anthology I, p.115). His boast was undeniable. His rule affected 80 million Europeans in the continental French empire and the satellite-states that fell under his sway during the Napoleonic Wars that followed the Revolutionary Wars and raged across Europe from 1800 to 1815.[2] In your set book Stendhal refers to him as 'the great conqueror' (p.150) and 'Napoleon the Conqueror' (p.118).

Yet Napoleon was more than warrior and conqueror. He was an organizer, administrator, legislator and modernizer. He 'rewrote the map of Europe for a time and set in motion processes that were to continue long after his fall' (Hampson, 1969, p.151). A recent commentator, Philip Dwyer, claims that Napoleon's continental empire 'embodies, to an even greater extent than the French Revolution, the passage of Ancien Régime Europe to the modern world. In this process, no one is more responsible for dragging Europe ... into the modern era than Napoleon' (Dwyer, 2001b, p.ix).

The 'Napoleonic phenomenon' fascinated contemporaries (including Napoleon himself), and has continued ever since to exert a powerful compulsion and to provoke discussion and reinterpretation. As Roland Gant says in his introduction to your set text (p.16):

> There is no end to the curiosity about him, to the distortion of the facts in books, the theatre and cinema, to the theorizing and romanticizing. Little corporal, great general, ruthless tyrant, brilliant legislator, vulgar Corsican upstart, in every role in which he is viewed there is basis for speculation and wonder.

The purpose of Units 7–8 is to introduce you to 'the Napoleonic phenomenon': to familiarize you with the main events in Napoleon's career, to encourage you to engage with the challenges involved in interpreting the man and his significance, and so far as possible to reach your own informed conclusions based on the evidence at your disposal.

---

[2] As well as further millions beyond: for example, in Britain and Russia.

## Stendhal's *A Life of Napoleon*

Your set text, and main source on Napoleon for the purposes of this course, is Stendhal's *Life of Napoleon*. Written in Milan between November 1817 and August 1818, this biography was not published in Stendhal's lifetime for reasons which you will explore. Indeed, it was published in full only in 1929. It first appeared in an English translation by Roland Gant in 1956, and this translation has been specially revised and annotated in a new edition for this course.

It is an unusual book, written in his early thirties by Henri Beyle, better known as the novelist Stendhal (1783–1842), author of *Scarlet and Black* (1830) and *The Charterhouse of Parma* (1839). In one respect it is unique. Of the hundreds of biographies of Napoleon, only one – Stendhal's – was written by a contemporary who actually served under him from 1800 to 1814, virtually throughout the Napoleonic era. Stendhal was present at Napoleon's victorious entries into Milan (1800), Berlin (1806), Vienna (1809) and Moscow (1812), as well as during the disastrous retreat from Moscow. In Stendhal's book, therefore, we see Napoleon partly through the eyes of a young man who witnessed many of the events which he described, formed his own impressions and drew his own, invariably interesting, conclusions.

You may like to read the book in its entirety. We hope you will be tempted to do so, but you are only required to read 54 chapters (listed at the beginning of these units) out of 87 (about 30,000 words out of 60,000 or roughly half the book). Feel free to read the linking chapters if you have time. Most chapters are only a paragraph or two in length, and the three longest chapters are only a dozen pages each. Where TMAs and exam questions relate to particular chapters, you will be alerted in advance.[3]

*A Life of Napoleon* contains a number of names, and Stendhal tends to refer to the more important of these by the imperial titles which Napoleon bestowed on his marshals and chief ministers. For example, his foreign minister Talleyrand usually appears as 'the Duke of Benevento', his chief of police – Fouché – as 'the Duke of Otranto', and so on. You do not need to know more than half-a-dozen of the main characters, since the only character who really matters is Napoleon himself. For ease of understanding, the set text provides brief explanations of who is who in the editorial footnotes, which gloss names and references requiring clarification and should provide all the further information you need. It also contains a chronology of the main events in Napoleon's career.

*A Life of Napoleon* should be an enjoyable read – Stendhal, after all, became a novelist. Occasionally his train of thought is a little hard to

---

[3] Chapters 36–9 and 41–2 (not compulsory reading) relate to Napoleon's fatal intervention in Spain, discussed in Video 2, band 1, *Goya*. Reference to brief extracts from these chapters is made in the AV Notes.

follow. But the book has pace, verve, pungent authorial comment and challenging judgements, which you are of course free to take issue with. Stendhal felt strongly and wrote forcefully. That does not mean he is necessarily 'right'. As he himself concedes in his preface: 'Since everyone has a definite idea about Napoleon, this *Life* cannot fully satisfy anyone' (p.20). Stendhal can also be ambiguous and even contradictory. Furthermore, as Pieter Geyl reminds us in *Napoleon: For and Against*: 'the historian is after all only a man sitting at his desk' (1965, p.18). In reaching your own conclusions about Napoleon – another objective of these units – you will have opportunities to test Stendhal's account against the evidence of other contemporary sources, including documents by or concerning Napoleon presented in Anthology I, and visual and other evidence included in or associated with this block.

Stendhal has links with other texts in the course. He was passionately fond of music, his favourite composer was Mozart, and his favourite opera was *Don Giovanni*. He wrote a *History of Painting in Italy* in 1817, and was a friend and critic of the artist Delacroix. He admired Goethe and Byron, whom he considered 'the greatest living poet' (Martineau, 1952, p.353). In 1816 he met Byron in Milan. 'I was ecstatic as I re-read *Childe Harold*,' he recalled, 'I loved Lord Byron' (Stendhal, 1962, p.197). He visited England and the Lake District. He described himself in 1818 as 'a furious romantic' (Hemmings, 1987, p.165). In 1823 he wrote a key book on Romanticism, revised in 1825 as *Racine and Shakespeare*. *A Life of Napoleon*, like its subject and its author, spans the Enlightenment and Romanticism and reflects both.

# 2   The Napoleonic phenomenon

## Images of Napoleon

'Everyone,' says Stendhal in his preface, 'has a definite idea about Napoleon' (p.20). Probably you have your own image, perhaps a variant of one popular in his own time and later: the little man with the famous cocked hat and grey great-coat (*redigote grise*, p.213), widely familiar from pictures, caricatures, statues, poems, novels and films.[4] Figures 7.11, 7.13, 7.14, 7.16 and the cover illustrations to this block and to your edition of *A Life of Napoleon* show some contemporary images.

What is strange is that we cannot be sure exactly what he looked like. No two likenesses of him are the same, and many of them, as you will see, appear to have been idealized. On the other hand, Stendhal, who

---

[4] For example, Tolstoy's *War and Peace* (1869), the film of the novel directed by Sergei Bondarchuk (1966), the film *Waterloo*, also directed by Bondarchuk (1970), starring Rod Steiger as Napoleon.

was an eyewitness, states that 'his face was beautiful, sometimes sublime' (p.35 footnote). As you may remember from Unit 1, the word 'sublime' had powerful emotional and aesthetic resonances in the period, and you may think that Stendhal's description is brought out in Figure 7.1 or in the cover illustration.

*Figure 7.1   François Gérard,* Napoleon as First Consul, *1803, 62 × 53 cm, Musée Condé, Chantilly. Photo: Giraudon/Bridgeman Art Library.*

*'... a superior mind full of romantic plans and passionately devoted to extraordinary undertakings' (LN, p.37).*

According to Stendhal, some of Napoleon's most famous portraits did not resemble him at all, and 'those by David and Canova' (the best-known painter and sculptor of the age) were 'the worst' (p.35). According to Stendhal the 'least bad portraits' included the bust by the sculptor Chaudet (Figure 7.12, p.66). What kind of 'image' of Napoleon does Stendhal set out to portray in his book?

**EXERCISE**   Read the quotation which forms the heading to chapter 1 of *A Life of Napoleon* (p.21). The quotation is from a funeral tribute by Bossuet, the leading French churchman under Louis XIV, to one of the king's greatest generals and military heroes, Louis, Prince de Condé (1621–86), known as 'the Great Condé'.

Why do you suppose Stendhal begins his first chapter with this quotation?

**DISCUSSION**   I suggest two main reasons.

1   He seeks to draw an implicit parallel between Condé, 'this great man and … the marvels of his life', and Napoleon, in Stendhal's eyes the greatest living Frenchman.

2   He wants to suggest that, like Bossuet, Stendhal may fail to measure up to the greatness of his subject.

Stendhal's overall aim, therefore, seems to be to emphasize Napoleon's greatness.

**EXERCISE**   Now read the first five sentences of chapter 1. What do they suggest about the book?

**DISCUSSION**   First, the book is a polemic: a defence of Napoleon against a 'slanderous' attack by Mme de Staël.

Second, in attempting to vindicate Napoleon, he, Stendhal, will have a hard task and will be swimming against a strong tide of reaction against Napoleon. Staël, 'the leading talent of the age', was also a rich and highly influential leader of society; and Napoleon had 'for the past four years' (that is, since 1814) been marked down for punishment by the **Great Powers** (Britain, Austria, Prussia and Russia) and banished, first to Elba and then to remote St Helena.

# Napoleon: between Enlightenment and Romanticism

Napoleon himself felt that his career resembled a work of fiction. 'What a novel my life has been' (*Quel roman que ma vie*), he reflected afterwards (quoted in Bruun, 1967, p.106). In his meteoric career, crammed with great and startling events, there were many elements common to Romantic fiction, poetry and art – and these elements feature in Stendhal's *Life*. First comes the rapid rise from obscurity to awesome heights of fame as conqueror, law-giver and master of Europe: 'I have pushed back the boundaries of greatness', as Napoleon declared (Anthology I, p.114). 'This man's whole life is a paean in praise of greatness of soul', Stendhal writes (LN, p.43). From these heights he fell to a tragic destiny as an outlawed exile. Napoleon's career, then, was felt – by himself and others – to resemble a Romantic novel with a hero and a drama acted out on a world stage, full of action, excitement, travel, exoticism, triumph and tragedy.

Napoleon also appeared to be 'the finest embodiment of human willpower', in the words of the German philosopher Schopenhauer, who met him (quoted in Geyl, 1965, p.349). This is another Romantic talisman: the outstanding individual shaping mighty events and reshaping the face of Europe with vast creative energy. 'What I am', Napoleon wrote in 1805, 'I owe to strength of will, character, application and daring' (Herold, 1955, p.43). At his height he seemed a kind of superman or demi-god: unstoppable, invincible, defying fate and death. He was not, of course, a demi-god, and his supreme faith in himself contained its own penalty. In Stendhal's words, 'Had he had any *self-doubt*, had he been able to hesitate, to ask for advice on Spain, for example, or about leaving Moscow earlier, he could not have had that *inflexible willpower* that can only come from extreme self-confidence' (LN, p.115 footnote).

In 1812, at the very summit of his power and prestige, he embarked on his Russian campaign. 'If I succeed in Russia, I shall be master of the whole world,' he declared (LN, p.158). There followed instead the epic catastrophe of the retreat from Moscow and its sequel: a succession of military defeats and 'frightful disasters' (LN, p.164), interspersed with some of his most brilliant victories, in which he 'frequently recovered as a general the genius of his early years' (LN, p.171). Within just over a year the great French empire and Napoleon's mastery of Europe were lost. Forsaken by his generals, he abdicated. Then came the extraordinary return from Elba, the Hundred Days, defeat at Waterloo, and the pathos of his final exile.

Napoleon in exile was often compared to a fallen Titan (in Greek mythology, a demi-god punished for disobeying Zeus, king of the gods). The comparison was made – Napoleon made it himself (Herold, 1955, p.281) – with Prometheus, the Titan who cherished (some say created) humankind, bringing from heaven the divine secret of fire, light and civilization, and who for his temerity was condemned by Zeus to be tied forever to a rock while an eagle or vulture gnawed at his liver.

All this (including the parallel drawn from classical mythology) is the stuff of Romanticism, and yet there is an underlying paradox. Napoleon's outlook was rooted in Enlightenment values: reason and 'common sense' (LN, p.131). He had an upbringing in mathematics, a profound respect for science, a colossal appetite for facts and figures, budgets and logistics; as Stendhal wrote, 'all decrees appertaining to organization, everything belonging to the domain of pure reason, if I may put it thus, proclaimed an outstanding genius' (p.117). Napoleon believed in orderly certainties, notably the essential rationality and uniformity of Europeans. He was the framer of a Europe-wide code of civil laws, the **Code Napoléon**, which he held to be universally applicable.

*a good administrator*

Napoleon was also 'imbued with Roman ideas' (LN, p. 53). He identified himself and France – the Great Nation (*la Grande Nation*) – with Roman military and cultural grandeur. This Roman sense of a civilizing mission, his classical tastes in literature, art and architecture, his declared preference for Voltaire over Rousseau, and his suppression in 1810 of an early manifesto of Romanticism, Mme de Staël's *On Germany,* also reflect his contempt for mysticism, woolly sentiment and vague idealism, which he dismissed contemptuously as 'metaphysics'. All this seems to ground Napoleon firmly in the eighteenth century in which he lived the first 30 years – the formative years – of his life.

At the same time his career was also shot through with a mystic faith in his own destiny, his 'star', which he believed he must follow to the end for better or worse. Offsetting his taste for the classical tragedies of Voltaire and the seventeenth-century playwrights Corneille and Racine was his Romantic enthusiasm for the rhapsodies of Ossian, the mythical bard of the Hebrides (LN, p.146), which he liked 'for the same reason that I like to hear the whisper of the wind and the waves of the sea' (Herold, 1955, p.155).

Napoleon's ambiguous position on the cusp of Enlightenment and Romanticism – between common sense and wild extravagance – is exemplified in certain remarks he made the day after he crowned himself emperor in 1804. Regretting that, compared to Alexander the Great, 'I come too late, nothing great remains to be done', Napoleon observed that Alexander had declared himself to be the son of Zeus, king of the gods. 'Well,' he continued, 'if I declared myself the son of the Eternal Father ... every fishwife would hoot when she saw me pass by' (Herold, 1955, p.49). What was in his mind when he made this comment? Insatiable ambition, restless yearning, the lure of antiquity, colossal egotism tempered by practicality seem to jostle uneasily together in Napoleon's joke, if it was a joke. Stendhal suggests that he was good-humoured but too sensitive to personal criticism to be a humourist (pp.139–40).[5] 'Had I succeeded,' Napoleon reflected from St Helena, 'I should have died with the reputation of the greatest man that ever existed. As it is, although I have failed, I shall be considered as an extraordinary man' (Anthology I, p.115). The word 'extraordinary' occurs again and again in the reactions to Napoleon, attesting to the sense of wonder and amazement that he inspired.

## The Romantics and Napoleon

As Roland Gant points out: 'Napoleon's contemporaries found just as much difficulty in grasping the essentials of his character and the breadth of his influence as we have today' (p.16). In his own age and well beyond the period covered in this course, Napoleon continued to be regarded as far and away the most remarkable man of his time, perhaps of all time. Contemporaries were mesmerized by his mystique, by what Stendhal called 'the magic of his being ... Everyone ... felt that he was a man above other men' (p.115). Moreover, what for us is history was for them actuality. They lived through it. For his admirers Napoleon was, in Stendhal's words, 'the *modern* hero' (p.118). Stendhal stressed 'the wholly *modern* genius of Napoleon' (p.89; emphasis added). Even when the experience was apparently at an end, with Napoleon's final exile, they could not get over what had happened and were constantly reliving and reappraising it. When Stendhal wrote his *Life*, Napoleon was still very much alive; indeed, Stendhal's Italian friend and critic, Giuseppe Vismara, observed that it was inappropriate to call the book a *Life* when its subject was still living (Stendhal, 1986, p.413). Napoleon, though out of sight at St Helena, was certainly not out of mind, but remained the object of ceaseless controversy. He was an 'extraordinary personage', as Richard Whately, author of *Historic Doubts Relative to Napoleon Buonaparte*, wrote in 1819, adding:

> We are still occupied in recounting the exploits, discussing the character, inquiring into the present situation, and even conjecturing as to the future prospects of Napoleon.

> (Whately, 1985, p.7)

Mme de Staël, who turned from adulation of Napoleon to determined opposition – 'the one French writer who dared to stand up to Napoleon' (Hemmings, 1987, p.121) – agreed that he was an 'extraordinary man' and underlined the enigmatic nature of his character in her *Reflections on the Main Events of the French Revolution*, published in 1818:

---

[5] Decrès, minister of the navy, who reports the episode, claimed that Napoleon spoke in earnest, and observed of him on this occasion: 'Mad, absolutely mad' (Bessand-Massenet, 1978, p.367). Napoleon frequently expressed his veneration for Alexander the Great and his regret that he had not made himself emperor of the east and conquered India.

His genius and his character may be interpreted in different ways. There is something enigmatic in that man which retains our curiosity. Everyone paints him in different colours, and may well be right, depending on his point of view ... Time will elucidate the various sides of his character.

(Anthology I, p.121)

Napoleon exerted a huge fascination in the Romantic period as the incarnation of 'genius', including evil genius: 'one of the incarnations of evil' (LN, p.164; see also Figure 7.16, p.82). This was as true of those whose feelings towards him were ambivalent or who became alienated as of his admirers. Beethoven, you may recall from Block 1, dedicated his Third Symphony – the 'Eroica' (heroic) – to Napoleon, 'to a great man', but scratched out the dedication in 1804 when Napoleon made himself emperor, and rededicated it 'to the *memory* of a great man' (Robbins Landon, 1970, p.93). Mme de Staël, herself a leading light in the development of French Romanticism, did not deny Napoleon's genius even while she deplored its consequences. Sir Walter Scott (1771–1832), whose novels had an enormous impact on European Romanticism, wrote a hostile but best-selling *Life* of Napoleon in 1827, which earned him a staggering £18,000. Scott 'sold Napoleon', Stendhal wrote acidly, but even Scott agreed that Napoleon 'was and will remain the greatest man of his time' (quoted in Bainbridge, 1995, p.9). The essayist and political radical William Hazlitt, author of an admiring biography of Napoleon (1830) and another acquaintance of Stendhal, was passionately moved by Napoleon's fall in 1815. Its impact was such, he recalled in heightened language in 1826, that 'with him all we who remained were "thrown into the pit", the lifeless bodies of men, and wore round our necks the collar of servitude' (quoted in Lean, 1970, p.263). For the French Romantics the obsession with Napoleon increased as time went on, transmuting historical truth into myth, legend and artistic inspiration. The painter Delacroix wrote in 1824: 'For the arts, the life of Napoleon is the epic of our age' (Brookner, 2000, p.20). Victor Hugo's poem of 1828 entitled 'He' underlined the obsessive attraction. Everyone knew who 'He' was:

Always He. Everywhere He. Ardent or cold,
His image ever dominates my thought.

(Hugo, 1985, p.532; trans. Lentin)

The Lake poets – Wordsworth, Coleridge and Southey – were likewise 'obsessed by the figure of Napoleon' (Bainbridge, 1995, p.8). Goethe met Napoleon on three occasions in 1808 and again in 1813, and evidently regarded these encounters as 'the most extraordinary experience of his life' (Ellis, 1997, p.204); for Goethe Napoleon was 'a demonic being, an indomitable character, the equal of the Greek demi-gods' (quoted in Martineau, 1976, p.30), ambiguous, problematical and ultimately 'incommensurable' (quoted in Ellis, 1997, p.204). The historian André Guérard describes Napoleon as 'the Romantic ideal incarnate: adventure, gigantic dreams, the Ego challenging destiny, and the world well lost' (1956, p.346). These aspects of Napoleon appealed greatly to Byron, most potent of all poets in his influence on European Romanticism. In Canto III of *Childe Harold's Pilgrimage* (written in 1816) Byron makes the point that Napoleon, even after his fall, remained an epoch-making historical phenomenon, paradox and enigma:

> Conqueror and captive of the earth art thou!
> She trembles at thee still, and thy wild name
> Was ne'er more bruited in men's minds than now
> That thou art nothing, save the jest of fame.

(Stanza 37)

## Stendhal and Napoleon

Between the ages of 16 and 30, from 1800 to 1814, Stendhal was employed in the imperial service. These impressionable years, and the personality of Napoleon, left an indelible mark on his outlook. When, in

*Figure 7.2   Edme Queneday,* Stendhal *(aged 24), 1807, drawing, Musée Stendhal, Grenoble. Photo: Studio Piccardy, Grenoble.*

*In 1822 Stendhal's cousin wrote of 'his fine forehead, lively and penetrating eye, sardonic mouth, plenty of character' (Romain Colomb, quoted in Roy, 1968, p.10; trans. Lentin).*

*'I am a furious romantic, that is to say I am for Shakespeare against Racine, for Lord Byron against Boileau' (Stendhal, 1818, quoted in Hemmings, 1987, p.165).*[6]

[6] Nicolas Boileau (1636–1711), neoclassical literary critic, author of *The Art of Poetry,*

1817 and 1818 during Napoleon's final exile, Stendhal wrote *A Life of Napoleon*, he was, as his Italian friend Vismara wrote, 'the historian of his own times' (LN, p.50 footnote), and his book, though focused on Napoleon, also sees him through the lens of post-Napoleonic perceptions. Stendhal says in chapter 1 that it 'is not, strictly speaking, a history – it is a historical account intended for the contemporary spectator of events' (p.21). That is to say, it discusses Napoleon for his wider significance in the history of France and Europe, viewed by a thoughtful observer who had both experienced the Napoleonic phenomenon at the time and looked back at it during the post-1815 reaction.

Throughout his life Stendhal shared the enthusiasm of the Romantics for Napoleon. In 1832 he wrote of 'Napoleon (whom I always adored)' (Stendhal, 1975, p.33). You should not assume, however, that Stendhal's attitude is one of unalloyed hero-worship. In 1837 he wrote: 'My love for Napoleon is the only passion remaining to me;' adding significantly, 'yet it does not prevent my seeing his faults and the petty weaknesses with which he can be reproached' (LN, p.19). He shows this ambivalence in his *Life of Napoleon*.

Stendhal's attitude to Napoleon was both engaged and detached, complex and nuanced. He was critical, often biting and cynically realistic, with a sardonic sense of humour. He invariably sought to be different, unconventional, paradoxical and original, sometimes to the point where, as his fellow novelist Prosper Mérimée noted in 1849, 'it was difficult to know what he thought of Napoleon. His almost invariable practice was to argue against whatever opinion was being advanced (Hemmings, 1966, p.112). Stendhal's pointed observations make you think and are worth thinking about. He is a rigorous analyst with the telling phrase and the illuminating generalization of an acute observer, with an independent mind steeped in the rationalism of the Enlightenment yet responsive to contemporary currents of Romanticism.

If you wish to read some or all of the selected chapters of Stendhal's *Life of Napoleon* now, feel free to do so. If you prefer to study more background material first, read on.

# 3   Napoleon on Napoleon – propagandist, image-maker, actor and 'chameleon'

Why read Stendhal? Why not let Napoleon, who left 60,000 letters and copious documents, speak for himself? In fact, we ask you to consider the Stendhal text together with a dozen brief examples of Napoleon's own testimony, including accounts with which Napoleon clearly intended to impress posterity (Anthology I, pp.114–18). You should examine the latter documents with particular care. Why? The answer is simply that often they are not to be trusted, and that to base a study of Napoleon on Napoleon's own utterances would risk succumbing, as so many have done, to his powerful and seductive propaganda. For not the least of his outstanding talents was a gift for public relations and self-presentation.

Throughout his career Napoleon was concerned, continually and obsessively, with his own prestige and reputation. Leaving aside his inner compulsions, his obvious and constant urge to dominate, impress and even to humiliate (Dwyer, 2001a, pp.132–5), Napoleon was always conscious of his origins and his essential vulnerability as an outsider and Corsican upstart, Napoleone Buonaparte,[7] who in 1804 quite literally crowned himself Emperor of the French, emphasizing the point that he was a self-made man. Unlike the hereditary dynasts elsewhere in Europe (notably the Habsburg Emperor Francis of Austria, the Hohenzollern King Frederick-William III of Prussia, the Romanov Emperor Alexander I of Russia, and indeed the Bourbon claimants to the French throne itself, the younger brothers of Louis XVI, refugees in England), Napoleon claimed that he had to justify his position and ensure his predominance in France and Europe by a continual spectacle of success, military and civilian. Even at the height of his fame, around 1812, he said privately:

> Five or six families are sharing the thrones of Europe, and they are pained to see a Corsican taking a seat on one of them. I cannot keep my place except by using force. I cannot accustom them to look upon me as an equal except by keeping them under my yoke. As soon as I cease to be feared, my empire is destroyed ... What would be an indifferent matter to a king of an old dynasty is very serious to me. I shall persist in this attitude so long as I live.

(Herold, 1955, p.241)

Napoleon's perceptions in this passage may be questioned and qualified. His sensitivity as an outsider may have been exaggerated or overplayed, consciously or unconsciously. He repeated the thought, and he followed it after the catastrophic Russian campaign of 1812, desperately fighting to prevent the disintegration of his continental empire. Whether Europe was ever willing to accept Napoleon's domination of an enlarged France is a matter of ongoing debate. What is certain is that his continual self-assertion, military aggression and territorial expansion engendered the successive European coalitions against him, and ultimately served to convince his enemies that there could be no lasting peace as long as he ruled. In France itself, his own ministers Talleyrand and Fouché reached

---

[7] Corsica, a possession of Genoa since 1347, was sold to Louis XV of France in 1768, a year before Napoleon's birth. Stendhal, who notes the first appearance in 1793 of Napoleon's surname in its French version (LN, p.26 footnote), states that Napoleon 'spoke neither French nor Italian accurately' (p.130).

this conclusion by 1810 or earlier, and began to negotiate secretly with the Allies.

The point here is that, for a variety of reasons (themselves matters of debate), Napoleon always kept a close eye on the formation of public opinion. 'Interested in propaganda as a means of self-aggrandizement as well as for furthering government policy, Napoleon kept the spotlight constantly on himself' (Holtman, 1967, p.163). Not only was he a legend in his own lifetime, but he himself assiduously cultivated and consciously shaped and reshaped that legend.

---

**EXERCISE**   To take a well-known early example of Napoleonic propaganda, consider the equestrian portrait of Napoleon crossing the Alps in 1800 by the foremost French artist of the day, Jacques-Louis David (see the cover illustration and Plate 9.8 in the Illustrations Book).

In a word, how would you describe the image of Napoleon which David intended to convey?

---

**DISCUSSION**   I would say that David's intention is to present Napoleon as *heroic*.

---

*Napoleon had it re-written 4 times.*

*NO!*

*It was Monnier*

*(Chandler)*

At Napoleon's request, David depicted Napoleon 'in calm pose on a fiery stallion' in a snowstorm (Michel and Lavoix, 1897, p.324). In fact, Napoleon crossed the Alps in fine weather on a mule. His aim was to drive the Austrians out of Italy, but he came close to defeat at the battle of Marengo and owed his victory to General Desaix, who was killed in action. This campaign was Napoleon's first military success after he took power as First Consul in 1799. David's picture was a key element in the creation of the Napoleonic legend, designed to justify his seizure and retention of power. (Napoleon had the role of the dead Desaix written out of the official record of the campaign.)

For historians of Napoleon, then, a central problem when considering his official version of events is to distinguish fact from fiction, propaganda from truth. Napoleon was adept in combining both in the images of himself which he helped to create and to spread across France and Europe through his close, active and purposeful control of the media: the press (including his own proclamations and military bulletins), art, architecture, public festivals and celebrations, and the theatre. This aspect of Napoleon's control of art and architecture is further explored in Audio 3, tracks 8–12, *Images of Napoleon* (which you are asked to listen to later in the units), and in Unit 9.

# Napoleon's self-projection as the bearer of enlightenment

Plate 7.1 in the Illustrations Book is an allegorical representation of 1810 demonstrating Napoleon's achievement as the bearer of enlightenment. The caption reads: 'To the mighty emperor who from the heart of the ruins is reviving laws, morals, victories and the arts.' In this engraving and in the *Mémorial de Sainte Hélène* which he dictated at St Helena (Anthology I, p.115) Napoleon represents his ambition as 'the grandest and noblest, perhaps, that ever was ... of establishing and consecrating at last the kingdom of reason and the full exercise, the complete enjoyment, of all human capabilities'. With this bold claim, Napoleon presents himself as a creative promoter of the Enlightenment tradition of reason and the champion of individual potential. At St Helena, as noted, he compared himself to Prometheus.[8]

**EXERCISE**      How does the image in Plate 7.1 bring out the message of the caption?

**DISCUSSION**
- The world is surmounted by an allegorical winged figure bearing the tablet of the law (probably the Code Napoléon – see Anthology I, p.115: 'a code of laws that will bear my name to the most distant posterity').

- Two similar figures, to left and right, trumpet Napoleon's achievements to the skies.

- A triumphal arch (similar to the Arc de Triomphe du Caroussel in the Tuileries, or the Arc de Triomphe de l'Étoile commissioned by Napoleon) celebrates his 'fifty pitched battles' and illustrates his promotion of the arts. (In 1810 Napoleon established a decennial art competition to celebrate his ten years in power. Winning entries included David's depiction of Napoleon's coronation, Plate 9.28.)

- Behind the globe, the rays of the sun dispel the dark clouds, a classic symbol of the Enlightenment.

Unusually, there is no image of Napoleon himself. Perhaps 'the mighty emperor' signalled in the caption is meant to be thought of as an aura, spirit or inspiration behind the enlightenment of the world, akin to a superhuman influence. The caption presents Napoleon as bringer of a

[8] See Herold, 1955, p.281. Goethe made the same comparison: 'Did he not, like Prometheus, bring light to mankind, moral enlightenment? ... He drew attention to the worth of every human being, to the role as citizen of each individual, his liberty, the danger of its loss and the need of its assertion ... He showed the people what they are capable of' (quoted in Lange, 1982, pp.201–2).

social, military and cultural renaissance created 'from the heart of the
ruins', by which expression is presumably meant the anarchy, violence
and squalor of the Revolution. The message of Plate 7.1 seems close to
Napoleon's claim in Anthology I, p.114: 'I have unscrambled chaos. I
have cleansed the Revolution.'

A gifted impresario and stage manager of his own actions with a strong
theatrical bent,[9] Napoleon, as Stendhal says, 'showed himself to be a
great tragic actor' (p.168), who in the many scenes of high drama across
his career wrote his own stirring lines and acted them out to the last.
After Waterloo, an outlaw in Europe, escape to America barred by the
British navy, he decided to seek asylum in England. See Figure 7.3 for
the carefully crafted letter which he sent to the Prince Regent, appealing
(with a classical allusion) to the magnanimity of Great Britain.

**EXERCISE**   Compare the reactions of Mme de Staël and Stendhal in the figure
caption to Napoleon's appeal to the Prince Regent.

**DISCUSSION**   Staël – liberal, Anglophile and constitutionalist – argues that it was not
for Napoleon to invoke the protection of English law: not only had he
been England's most persistent enemy, but no one, according to her, had
treated his own laws more arbitrarily. (Staël herself had been exiled at
his order.)

Stendhal argues that Napoleon's dramatic appeal to Britain for
magnanimity received a shabby and ungenerous response.

## Napoleon's 'justifications from St Helena'

Napoleon contributed particularly energetically to his legend after his fall.
In exile at St Helena, he dictated his thoughts and reminiscences (see
Figure 7.4), factually a more or less accurate record of his past, but
coloured by the glosses which he placed retrospectively on his own role
and intentions. Stendhal rightly calls these accounts 'his justifications
from Saint Helena' (p.216). They were afterthoughts. Napoleon was 're-
perusing' (as Las Cases put it) or re-inventing himself in them and
recasting his own image. They were partly a way of passing the time:
idleness was unendurable to this quintessential man of action for whom
'work is my element' (quoted in Fisher, 1971, p.148). In addition, until
early in 1819 Napoleon believed that the memoirs might assist his return
to Europe (he hoped for a change of government in Britain and
honourable retirement in England in the style of a country gentleman).

[9] As First Consul Napoleon went to the theatre twice weekly (Lentz, 1999, p.421).

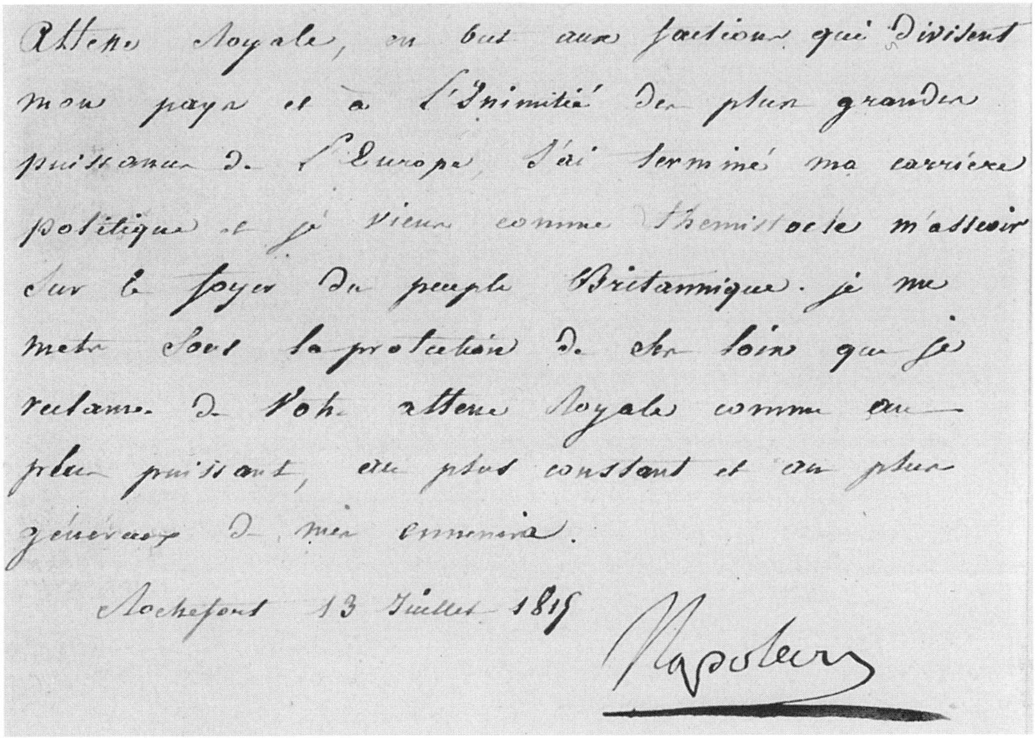

Altesse Royale, en butte aux factions qui divisent
mon pays et à l'inimitié des plus grandes
puissances de l'Europe, j'ai terminé ma carrière
politique et je viens comme Thémistocle m'asseoir
sur le foyer du peuple Britannique. je me
mets sous la protection de ses lois que je
réclame de Votre Altesse Royale comme au
plus puissant, au plus constant et au plus
généreux de mes ennemis.

Rochefort 13 Juillet 1815

Napoleon

*Figure 7.3 Napoleon's letter to the Prince Regent, 13 July 1815, The Royal Collection, Windsor. Photo: © 2002 Her Majesty Queen Elizabeth II.*

*The letter reads: 'Royal Highness, Pursued by the factions which divide my country and by the hostility of the greatest powers of Europe, I have ended my political career, and I come, like Themistocles,*[10] *to sit at the hearth of the British people. I place myself under the protection of its laws, which I claim from Your Royal Highness as the most powerful, most constant and most generous of my enemies. Rochefort 13 July 1815. Napoleon.'*[11]

*'Bonaparte, who for ten years had roused the world against the freest country [Britain], ... placed himself in her hands. He, who for ten years had outraged her every day, appealed to her generosity. Finally he, who spoke of the laws only with contempt, who so lightly gave orders for arbitrary imprisonment, invoked the liberty of the English, and sought to place himself under its protection: Oh, if he had only granted France that liberty, neither he nor the French would find themselves at the mercy of the victors' (Mme de Staël,* Reflections on the Main Events of the French Revolution, *1818, in Anthology I, p.120).*

*'Napoleon, who had appealed to the greatly vaunted generosity of the English people, was imprisoned upon a rock' (LN, p.100).*

[10] Themistocles (fifth century BCE) defended Greece from Persia, but finally took refuge at the court of King Artaxerxes of Persia. The episode is described in Plutarch's life of Themistocles.

[11] The letter went unanswered. The British government, with the agreement of the other allied powers (Russia, Austria, Prussia), declared Napoleon to be their 'prisoner' and exiled him to St Helena.

More significantly, however, he sought to immortalize his reputation with the slants which he chose to place on it. The Count de Las Cases, one of his entourage in exile, took down his dictation between 1815 and 1816 and published it in 1823 as the *Mémorial de Sainte Hélène: Journal of the Private Life and Conversations of the Emperor Napoleon at Saint Helena*. The *Mémorial* became one of the bestsellers of the nineteenth century.[12] Another best-selling account of Napoleon's reminiscences was published by his Irish doctor, Barry O'Meara, as *Napoleon in Exile or a Voice from St Helena* (1822). Napoleon intended posterity to be swayed by his eloquent self-advocacy, and when approaching these eminently readable books (excerpts from which you will now consider), the reader should be warned: open with care.

**EXERCISE**

Now read 'Napoleon on his achievements, 1816' and 'Napoleon on his achievements, 1817' (Anthology I, pp.114–15). 'Is there any point on which I could be attacked and on which a historian could not take up my defense?' he asks (p.114). How far does Napoleon admit to any faults?

**DISCUSSION**

He admits on p.115 to 'the faults I have committed', without, however, saying what they are.

In the first document he cites issues 'on which I could be attacked', namely:

- his 'despotism' and limitation of freedom;

- his love of war and ambition 'to set up a universal monarchy' (also mentioned in the next document).

But he raises these charges (which were indeed and remain the main charges against him) only to rebut them one by one, giving his explanation in each case. The only fault he acknowledges is 'ambition', but he defends it as 'the grandest and noblest ... that ever was' (p.115). He also claims that his rise to power was 'unaccompanied by any crime' (p.115). Napoleon thus explicitly denies the main charges commonly laid against him, and insists that historians will 'take up my defense'. 'In spite of all the libels,' he told O'Meara, 'I have no fear whatever about my fame. Posterity will do me justice' (p.115).

---

[12] The *Mémorial de Sainte Hélène* was the inspiration of Julien Sorel, the hero of Stendhal's novel *Scarlet and Black* (1830). Stendhal had access to early versions of the *Mémorial,* smuggled out of St Helena, when writing *A Life of Napoleon*.

*Figure 7.4   P. Baquoy,* Napoleon at St Helena Dictating his Memoirs to the Son of Las Cases, c.*1825, engraving, Heber Mardon Collection, Devon Local Studies Library, Exeter. Photo: courtesy of Devon Library and Information Services.*

> *Napoleon: But what can we do in that desolate place?*
> *Las Cases: Sire, we will live on the past; there is enough of it to satisfy us. Do we not enjoy the life of Caesar and that of Alexander? We shall possess still more – you will re-peruse yourself, Sire!*
> *Napoleon: Be it so. We will write our memoirs. Yes, we must work; for work is the scythe of time. After all, a man must fulfil his destiny. That is my grand doctrine: well, let mine too be accomplished.*

> *(Conversation aboard HMS* Bellerophon, *2 August 1815, adapted from Las Cases, 1999, vol.1, p.57; trans. Lentin)*

*'Posterity will do me justice' (Napoleon at St Helena, conversation with O'Meara, 3 March 1817, in Anthology I, p.115).*

32

BLOCK 2   THE NAPOLEONIC PHENOMENON

# Napoleon's wars – aggressive or defensive?

EXERCISE   Now examine Figures 7.5 and 7.6 to give yourself a clear idea of the geographical extent of Napoleon's conquests up to 1812.

*Figure 7.5   Map showing principal Napoleonic battles, from Michael Broers,* Europe under Napoleon 1799–1815, *Edward Arnold (Publishers) Limited, 1996.*

*The Napoleonic Wars are reckoned to have caused 916,000 French deaths alone, a casualty rate of 38 per cent of men aged between 20 and 25, excluding possibly half a million men missing (Sutherland, 1985, p.423, Castelot, 1989, vol.2, p.897). Napoleon left France a smaller country in 1815 than he found it in 1799.*

*'I have fought fifty pitched battles, almost all of which I have gained' (Napoleon at St Helena, conversation with O'Meara, in Anthology I, p.115).*

*'I was led to it [the conquest of Europe] step by step by our very enemies' (Napoleon at St Helena, conversation with Las Cases, in Anthology I, p.115).*

*'Napoleon was engaged in several wars which shed torrents of blood, but in none of them, with the exception of the war in Spain, was he the aggressor ... Posterity will say that it was in repelling the attacks of his neighbours that he expanded his empire' (LN, p.217).*

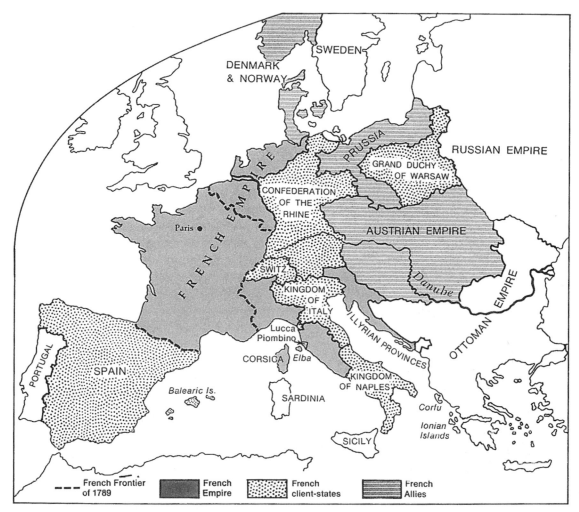

*Figure 7.6 Map showing Napoleonic Europe in 1812, from Ernest John Knapton,* Revolutionary and Imperial France 1750–1815, *Scribner, New York, 1972.*

The French empire at its fullest extent in 1812 consisted of 130 departments with a population of around 44 million. Including client-states (several ruled by the Bonapartes) and other dependent states, Napoleon controlled some 80 million people.

'Ah, it was a pretty Empire. I had eighty-three million human beings to govern' (Napoleon at St Helena, in Gourgaud, 1932, p.121).

'What, then, did he offer to the states which he sought to subjugate? Was it freedom, power, riches? No, it was he, always he' (Mme de Staël, 1818, in Anthology I, p.119).

'Madame de Staël ... [sees] in this only misfortune for the human race; the truth is just the opposite' (LN, p.61).

Despite the successive coalitions mounted against him, Napoleon was master of Europe (though never of Britain) for almost ten years. Nelson's victory at Trafalgar (1805) ensured Britain's naval supremacy, which made it impossible for Napoleon to invade England – though Stendhal argues that a bold attempt might have succeeded (p.78). On the Continent, by contrast, there was no stopping Napoleon in central and eastern Europe until 1812. One after another, the Great Powers buckled under his stupendous victories. In 1805 he smashed Austria at Austerlitz and knocked Russia out of the coalition. In 1806, at Jena, he smashed Prussia. The battles of Eylau and Friedland in 1807 secured a Franco-Russian alliance at Tilsit. From 1807 to 1812 the French empire was at its height and Napoleon seemed unchallengeable. What drained and undermined the French empire was his intervention in Spain in 1808 – the 'Spanish ulcer' or 'wasps' nest', as he admitted later – and his invasion of Russia in 1812.

In 1812 the French empire included Belgium, Luxembourg, the Rhineland, Holland, part of northern Germany bordering the North Sea, part of Switzerland, and a large part of northern and central Italy. All these territories were annexed to France and divided into departments (see Figure 7.8, p.55), as was part of the eastern seaboard of the Adriatic (the Illyrian Provinces).

Closely tied to the French empire was a ring of client-states, each furnished with a French-style administration (and several ruled by a member of the Bonaparte family): the Confederation of the Rhine (including the kingdoms of Westphalia, Württemberg, Saxony and Bavaria, and the Grand Duchies of Berg and Baden); the kingdoms of Italy and Naples and the Grand Duchy of Warsaw. Spain may also be considered a client-state, though only parts of it were under French control during the guerrilla war which raged throughout the French occupation of 1808–14.

Allied to the French empire were Austria and Prussia, nominally independent but with modified frontiers and under French occupation. The kingdom of Denmark and Norway was also a French ally. By 1812, then, almost the whole of Europe was under Napoleon's control, direct or indirect.

Some of Napoleon's claims in the documents 'on his achievements' that you have read are highly contentious. Note, however, that Stendhal accepts uncritically Napoleon's explanation of his wars and his expansion of the French empire as acts of self-defence. Only in Spain, Stendhal says, was Napoleon the aggressor. Some French historians have shared this view. Albert Sorel, in his multi-volume *L'Europe et la Révolution Française* (*Europe and the French Revolution*, 1885–1904), argued that the Great Powers, and particularly Britain, refused to accept the expanded France of the republic which Napoleon took over in 1799, with its 'natural frontiers' and in particular its incorporation of Belgium. Sorel also agreed with Napoleon's claim in 1816 that throughout the

Napoleonic Wars, 'I was always on the defensive' (Anthology I, p.114). This line is followed by Jacques Bainville in his classic biography of Napoleon (1938). Few modern historians accept this interpretation (see Dwyer, 2001a, pp.118–35). Rather, like many of his contemporary critics, they blame Napoleon's apparently insatiable desire to 'be considered as an extraordinary man' (Anthology I, p.115), seeking by his conquests to rank with Julius Caesar and Charlemagne. Napoleon claimed that his successive military strikes were defensive, but they invariably provoked renewed resistance, not the durable peace which he promised.

Consideration of these two Anthology documents also serves to emphasize both the variety of historical interpretation and the fact that any document which Napoleon intended the public to see should be treated with special caution because 'he had the ability to make his contemporaries see in him what he wanted them to see, although the images were often contradictory' (Alexander, 1995, p.40). In both documents the contradictory images are of Napoleon, on the one hand, as dictator, warmonger and conqueror of Europe and, on the other hand (as in Plate 7.1), as upholder of law and order, whose mastery of Europe was 'merely the fortuitous result of circumstances' (Anthology I, p.115) and the fault of France's enemies.

> Yes, the Great Napoleon
> Is a great chameleon

wrote the poet Théodore Desorgues in 1804, who was promptly sent without charge or trial to a lunatic asylum, where he died four years later (Godechot, 1968, p.637).[13] His point evidently hit the mark. And his incarceration also suggests something about the character of the Napoleonic regime.

#  The truth about Napoleon

## Stendhal, sources and subjectivity

In this section we consider the question: how does Stendhal ascertain the truth about Napoleon? (For that matter, how does any biographer or historian gain reliable information about a figure from the past?)

**EXERCISE**   Read Stendhal's preface, p.20. Taking the preface paragraph by paragraph, consider what it suggests about Stendhal's intentions.

---

[13] De Sade was similarly put away between 1801 and his death in 1814 as the author of the pornographic novel *Justine*.

**DISCUSSION**      **Paragraph one**

- Stendhal begins by indicating his wide reading of the sources and claims that all he has done is to base his book on selective quotations from them. He seems to be implying that by being based on a large number of available sources, his book is a reliable account.

(In fact, the books which he consulted total around 20, though they themselves often quote from other sources, so the actual total of sources is higher, though not the 200–300 authors suggested.)

**Paragraph two**

- He says that the biography cannot please everyone, 'since everyone has a definite idea about Napoleon', with which Stendhal's account may not accord and hence may not ring true; equally it may irritate or bore his readers.

Stendhal here implicitly brings out something applicable to every biographer or historian: the inevitable element of *subjectivity*. To a greater or lesser extent, a biography always reflects the author as well as its subject. A historian is not merely a dispassionate chronicler of events. By selection, ordering, highlighting and analysis of the available material, by the very choice of words, historians necessarily fashion a particular version or image of the subject, bringing to it their own point of view, interpretation and bias.

**Paragraphs three and four**

- Stendhal states that fuller evidence on Napoleon than that available in 1818 will appear in time with the publication of the memoirs of 'famous people', that is, people who played a leading role in Napoleon's career.

Thus in his preface Stendhal accepts the *provisional* nature of his biography. It cannot convey the whole truth about Napoleon until all the source material is available, when future historians will need to revise the view of Napoleon accordingly.[14] Furthermore, while historians writing today are probably in possession of most of the existing sources on Napoleon, because of the element of subjectivity inherent in any

---

[14] Stendhal includes the memoirs of General Caulaincourt among the key documents available to future historians. Caulaincourt's memoirs, which were not published until 1933, are an important source on Napoleon in the years 1812–14. Among other facts, Caulaincourt records Napoleon's attempted suicide after his first abdication in April 1814. Other important sources published later include the memoirs of Generals Gourgaud and Bertrand, who accompanied Napoleon to St Helena, published respectively in 1899 and 1949–59. Gourgaud recorded that Napoleon intended to resume his dictatorship if he had won at Waterloo. Gourgaud and Bertrand record his expression of sceptical views on religion.

biography, the definitive history – the last word about Napoleon – can never be written. There is always something new to say.

This is borne out by the incessant flood of publications on Napoleon. The historian Jean Tulard reckoned in 1977 that more books and articles had been written on Napoleon than the number of days that had elapsed since his death (1977, p.14), and it is true that scarcely a year goes by without at least one new book on the subject. Witness such books as Pieter Geyl, *Napoleon: For and Against* (1965), a study of French historians on Napoleon; Geoffrey Ellis, *Napoleon* in the series 'Profiles in Power' (1997); R.S. Alexander, *Napoleon* in the series 'Reputations' (2001); and the collection edited by Philip Dwyer entitled *Napoleon and Europe* (2001b). As Pieter Geyl says at the end of his book: 'the argument goes on' (p.400).

**EXERCISE**   Finally, consider the quotation at the start of the preface. The lines, from a Latin poem by an obscure English writer, celebrate the coming to power in Britain of William III (William of Orange, r.1688–1702). Can you suggest its relevance to *A Life of Napoleon*?

**DISCUSSION**   Stendhal is implicitly drawing a comparison between William and Napoleon. Both were foreigners, outsiders and soldiers who seized power with the help of the army and justified that seizure in terms of 'the preservation of liberty'. William, a Dutchman, invaded England and seized the throne in 1688 with only a dubious claim to it. Napoleon, a Corsican, seized power in a *coup d'état* in 1799 (known as the 18th Brumaire), becoming First Consul, and then emperor in 1804. Both were military heroes; both were acclaimed for saving freedom. William's admirers said that by the 'Glorious Revolution' of 1688 he saved Britain from absolutist tyranny; Napoleon's claimed that he saved the achievements of the French Revolution from Jacobin extremists, on the one hand, and counter-revolutionary royalists, on the other. Both men ruled for 14 years.

## Sources and their reliability

The historian's first duty is to get the facts right. Let us turn to the facts about Napoleon.

**EXERCISE**   Now read the first document in the extracts on Napoleon (Anthology I, pp.104–5) for an overview of Napoleon's career. Also consult the chronology in Stendhal's *Life of Napoleon*. It may be worth taking time to make sure you have a basic grasp of the main events. You may also find it helpful to consult the maps in Figures 7.5, 7.6 and 7.8 (pp.32, 33 and 55).

How do we know the facts about Napoleon, or anyone in the past? We depend on the evidence of primary sources. Broadly speaking, a **primary source** is a human record which bears witness to a contemporaneous historical event. Normally, for historians, a primary source is a written document (for example, Napoleon's letter to the Prince Regent reproduced in Figure 7.3, or the other contemporary documents by or concerning Napoleon published in the Anthology). Stendhal himself uses a variety of primary sources and, when he draws on his own recollections of Napoleon, produces a primary source of his own. Other primary sources include contemporary artefacts: for example, portraits, busts and medallions of Napoleon.

A **secondary source** is an account, based on primary sources, by someone (the historian) who has not necessarily witnessed the event in question. Most biographies of Napoleon, and all modern studies on him, are secondary sources. Stendhal's *Life of Napoleon,* unusually, is a hybrid work: it is essentially a secondary source inasmuch as it depends on primary sources; it also partakes of the nature of a primary source when Stendhal relates what he himself saw or heard.

The existence or discovery of a primary source, however, is only the beginning of the historian's search for the facts. The usefulness of a primary source – namely, the quality of the evidence it provides – depends on its accuracy and reliability. How reliable are the primary sources on Napoleon? In 1819 the question was put by Richard Whately in his *Historical Doubts Relative to Napoleon Buonaparte*, from which you have just read an extract.

Richard Whately was an Oxford don who later became Anglican Archbishop of Dublin. As a Christian, his purpose in *Historical Doubts* was to question the sceptical philosophy of David Hume, which you studied in Block 1. He does so by arguing that the evidence for Napoleon's career is no more credible in itself than the evidence for the events recorded in the Old Testament or the miracles recorded in the New Testament, the truth of which Hume had cast doubt on in his essay, 'Of miracles' (1748). Whately argued that, because of the variety of contradictory accounts and opinions about Napoleon and the inherent improbability of the alleged events – the story is too fantastic to be true – not only is it hard to be sure about the details of Napoleon's career (and harder still to be sure of his 'motives and conduct'), but even the evidence for Napoleon's very *existence* is suspect! Of course, Whately is being ironic: he does not really believe that Napoleon did not exist, but he does prompt the reader to take a critical attitude towards the evidence. By a curious coincidence, three years earlier at St Helena, Napoleon himself, speculating on his own historical reputation, made the same general point as Whately.

## 'Historical truth' – 'an agreed-upon fiction'?

Now read the second document (Anthology I, pp.105–6). What is the main point Napoleon is making?

Napoleon voices scepticism not about his own existence but about the reality of 'historical fact' generally, in view of the unreliability and inadequacy of the evidence and the conflicting accounts given by different sources. 'Historical truth', he says, is no more than 'an agreed-upon fiction'.

Think about Napoleon's definition of 'historical truth'. Do you agree that it is 'an agreed-upon fiction'?

It may certainly be 'very difficult', as Napoleon says, to establish the truth about a historical fact – that is, an event that took place in the past. (For example, consider the suspicious deaths in captivity in 1804 of the conspirators against Napoleon, General Pichegru and the Englishman, Captain Wright, discussed by Stendhal in chapter 25. It was widely rumoured that Napoleon had them secretly murdered.) In order to establish what really happened, we depend on primary sources, the evidence of eyewitnesses who saw or heard the event for themselves. We must then assess the reliability of that evidence. As Napoleon says, even when witnesses are unanimous, their evidence may still be mistaken, so that 'if, later on, there is a consensus, this is only because there is no one left to contradict' (p.105). So the truth, or the whole truth, about a historical fact may never be known, may 'remain in eternal litigation' for lack of evidence or, conversely, may be misapprehended from 'the flood of memoirs, diaries, anecdotes, drawing-room reminiscences' (p.105), which may or may not be accurate.

How convincing do you find Napoleon's scepticism about historical truth? Let us consider the question further.

## Was Napoleon murdered?

An example of this 'eternal ligitation', a historical controversy still current today, ironically, surrounds Napoleon's own death in 1821. Napoleon is traditionally thought to have died of stomach cancer related to an ulcer or hepatitis (Tulard, 1977, p.453; Markham, 1963, pp.255–6); but theories of arsenical poisoning, accidental (through the inhalation of arsenic from the wallpaper of his bedroom) or deliberate (through the administration of poison in his wine or medicine) have been frequently revived (see Richardson, 1974; Weider and Hapgood, 1982; Weider and Forshufvud, 1995; Maury and Candé-Montholon, 2000).[15] Stendhal himself alludes to poisoning – see p.100. The point is that the exact cause of Napoleon's death cannot be stated with absolute certainty for lack of reliable evidence.

*So why write the book?*

Knowledge of the facts about Napoleon, then, generally depends, first, on the availability of the evidence and, second, on its reliability. Stendhal agreed about availability: 'Fifty years hence, the history of Napoleon will have to be rewritten every year' (p.20) and 'the whole truth about Bonaparte cannot possibly be known for at least a century' (p.46) when more evidence becomes available. Even then, as Napoleon argues about reliability, 'what if they [the witnesses] are prompted by bad faith, self-interest and bias?' (Anthology I, p.106).

All these reservations about primary sources are amply justified, but what they boil down to is that all relevant sources should be approached *critically,* not that, given adequate evidence, it is impossible to establish objective facts, or what Napoleon calls 'material facts' or 'true truths'.

## Assassination attempt on Napoleon in 1809 – fact or fiction?

Let us take another example. After his victory at Wagram (July 1809), Napoleon was master of Austria. On 12 October he wrote from Vienna to inform his minister of police, Fouché, that an attempt on his life had just been made.

**EXERCISE**   Now read Napoleon's letter to Fouché (Anthology I, p.110). Assuming that the document is authentic (that is, that it is an accurate translation of a genuine letter from Napoleon to Fouché), can we be certain that the facts as told by Napoleon (and repeated by Stendhal, LN, p.85) are true? What do you think?

**DISCUSSION**   Without corroborative evidence, we cannot be absolutely certain. Napoleon could have made the whole thing up. This, however, seems

[15] These authors investigate the theory that Napoleon was poisoned by Count Montholon, a member of his entourage at St Helena and an alleged Bourbon agent. Napoleon's doctor, O'Meara, diagnosed hepatitis in October 1817, and was expelled from St Helena by the governor, Sir Hudson Lowe, in May 1818. In an official report he pointed out that hepatitis was endemic at St Helena and expressed the opinion that Napoleon's life was 'endangered by a longer residence' there. On his return to England, he hinted that Lowe had orders to hasten Napoleon's death. He was court-martialled and dismissed from the navy (Markham, 1963, pp.238–9).

inherently unlikely. Why should he relate to his chief of police a sensational fabrication which could serve no obvious purpose and <u>could easily have been exposed</u>? There must have been eyewitnesses present 'during parade' on 12 October 1809, who could readily confirm whether or not an attempt on his life had been made, including, according to Stendhal (p.85), Marshal Berthier (the Prince of Neuchâtel), Napoleon's chief of staff.

*'fanaticism'*

---

Moreover, if we consider Stendhal's version of events, there is another reason to accept that there was an assassination attempt. Stendhal must have obtained his account from somewhere (though he does not here cite his source). We know that he was stationed at Vienna at the time (Martineau, 1950, p.102), so he might have witnessed it himself, though this seems unlikely since he does not say so. We may therefore infer that he learned of it from some other source. This cannot have been Napoleon's letter to Fouché, which was confidential and not published until long after. There must therefore have been a second source. This again suggests that the event really happened or at least that independent evidence of it existed.

The next Anthology document, from General Rapp's memoirs (published in 1823), provides just such an independent source, which, with some minor discrepancies, confirms the main facts retailed by Napoleon. Assuming that Rapp's account is accurate, we learn among other things that, besides Rapp, two marshals and two generals, including Berthier (this confirms Stendhal's account), and also Savary, Napoleon's future minister of police, were present at Napoleon's interrogation of the would-be assassin, Friedrich Staps. So the unlikely hypothesis that Napoleon invented the incident may be dismissed.

The purpose of this digression is simply to show that, provided reliable evidence exists, we can establish that a particular event took place. Nor can it be denied that what Napoleon calls 'material facts' – the principal events of his career – are well established: that he fought some 50 battles, made himself emperor in 1804, invaded and retreated from Russia in 1812 with huge losses,[16] lost the battle of Waterloo in 1815, was exiled to St Helena and died there in 1821. There is plenty of evidence to establish the truth of all these assertions. These facts are 'incontrovertible'. No one can deny them.

What Napoleon argued in the document on pp.105–6 and Whately on p.104 were deliberate paradoxes, not meant by either man to be taken literally. Whately did not really doubt the fact of Napoleon's existence,

---

[16] Contemporary artefacts in the form of medals, buttons and scraps of uniform adhering to 2,000 skeletons, unearthed in 2001 in Vilna, Lithuania, prove these to be the remains of soldiers of the *Grande Armée* who perished during the retreat from Moscow (see *History Today*, vol.52, no.7, July 2002, p.10).

any more than Napoleon doubted the fact of his achievements, of which indeed he boasts on p.115, confidently claiming that 'the truth will be known'. Far from considering the facts to be 'an agreed-upon fiction', he said to Las Cases on 21 October 1816: 'The memory I leave behind consists of *facts* that mere words cannot destroy' (Anthology I, p.117; emphasis added).

If the main facts can be established with reasonable certainty, however, Napoleon's comments about the difficulty of establishing the *motives* for his actions – the reasons why he took certain decisions (his 'moral intent' or 'true intention', as he called it) – are more valid. This, indeed, is almost always to a greater or lesser extent a matter of inference by the historian (including Stendhal), depending partly on his 'individual way of thinking', in other words, his particular viewpoint and personal judgement. Why, for example, did Napoleon invade Russia in 1812? (Stendhal discusses this in chapters 55 and 56.) As Napoleon says: 'Suppose I have given an order: who can read the bottom of my thought, my true intention?' (Anthology I, p.106). And yet this is just what historians do try to do; for the state of a man's mind, however elusive, is as much a fact as his physical state.[17] And that is what Stendhal tried to do, to read Napoleon's mind, when he felt the evidence allowed. In one episode of Napoleon's Spanish policy, for example, he writes: 'In such a state of anxiety man cannot simulate, and it was possible to see deep into the heart and mind of the emperor' (p.91).

To sum up: while we may agree with Napoleon that 'the *true truths* are very difficult to ascertain in history' and that historians should weigh their sources with caution and scepticism (not least some of Napoleon's own accounts, and particularly his 'justifications from St Helena'), nonetheless historical truth does exist. We may also agree that the interpretation of character and intention, though equally – indeed more – 'difficult to ascertain', is also a proper and necessary object of historical enquiry. It is, of course, central to the writing of biography.


# 5   Stendhal's *A Life of Napoleon*


## Stendhal in the Napoleonic era

Henri Beyle (Stendhal) was born in Grenoble in the Dauphiné in 1783, the son of a lawyer. His mother, to whom he was devoted, died when he was seven. Brought up by his aunt and his father, both staunchly Catholic and royalist, and both of whom he loathed, he was precocious

---

[17] Napoleon suffered from retention of urine at Borodino and from haemorrhoids at Waterloo. It is sometimes suggested that these affected his concentration and hence the outcome of the battles.

(1793)

and rebellious, professing himself a Jacobin at ten years of age and exulting at the execution of Louis XVI. From 1796 to 1799 he was educated at the École Centrale in Grenoble (founded under a revolutionary decree of 1795 which introduced free education in France), becoming an enthusiast for the views of the eighteenth-century Enlightenment *philosophes* and a pronounced anticlerical. A prize-winning mathematician, he went to Paris at the age of 16 in 1799, arriving just after Napoleon's *coup d'état* of 18th Brumaire. His father wished him to take the entrance examination for the École Polytechnique (the great engineering school, also established under the Revolution), but he refused.

*[margin handwritten note: Why does Stendhal feel the need to write: "A Life of Napoleon".]*

A distant cousin, the highly placed soldier Pierre Daru, found him a position in the War Office, where he worked under Daru as a clerk. In 1800 he accompanied Daru to northern Italy, following Napoleon in his celebrated crossing of the Alps. Daru obtained for him a commission as a second lieutenant of Dragoons. Italy enchanted him, but he resigned his commission and returned to Paris in 1802. In 1806 he re-entered the army as an officer in the Commissariat when, again under the patronage of Daru (now Intendant-General of the *Grande Armée*), he joined Daru in Berlin shortly after Napoleon's victory at Jena. His career made rapid progress. He participated in the military administration of parts of the newly created satellite-kingdom of Westphalia and in 1809 was sent on a mission to Austria. In 1810 he was appointed as one of the 'auditors' or secretaries to the Council of State, Napoleon's supreme consultative body. The auditors were the seedbed of Napoleon's administrative elite, and Stendhal cherished hopes – unrealized – of becoming a prefect and a baron. In 1812 he served in the Russian campaign as a member of the supply corps, taking part in the retreat from Moscow. He served again in Austria in 1813, witnessed the battle of Bautzen in Saxony, and was sent to his home town of Grenoble to assist in the defence of the Dauphiné until Napoleon's first abdication in 1814, when he left France for Milan. He was 31.

*[margin handwritten note: verges on 'hagiography'!?]*

## The 'moment' of Stendhal's *A Life of Napoleon*

We raised earlier the question of subjectivity in the writing of history. All historians are to some degree affected by their background, political views, likes and dislikes. It may also be important – in Stendhal's case it *is* important – to note the 'moment' of writing: to consider what was going on at the time that may have influenced the writer and coloured his account.

### Europe after Napoleon

Stendhal wrote *A Life of Napoleon* in Milan between 1817 and 1818. The Hundred Days and Waterloo were recent, shattering events for Europe.

Their shock waves still resounded across a continent whöse frontiers the **Congress of Vienna** (1814–15) had just redrawn and many of whose former rulers it had restored in order to prevent a repetition of the Napoleonic phenomenon (see Figure 7.15, p.76, showing Europe in 1815 after the Congress of Vienna). Napoleon was still very much in the minds of the French and Europeans generally, sympathizers and enemies alike. Curiosity about him abounded. In October 1816 Byron met Stendhal in Milan and plied him with questions on Napoleon.

Napoleon himself was in his second year of exile. He had not yet lost hope of returning to Europe; nor was the possibility discounted in Europe (Mme de Staël alludes to it in Anthology I, p.120). His banishment was confirmed by the Great Powers at the Congress of Aix-la-Chapelle in November 1818 precisely because they continued to fear, and with reason, the power of his name and reputation, and his potential to set Europe by the ears yet again. His escape from Elba in 1815 had, after all, cost the lives of over 60,000 allied soldiers alone at Waterloo (Thornton, 1968, p.56). The Congress formally endorsed Tsar Alexander I's description of Napoleon as 'the power of the Revolution concentrated in one individual' (Aubry, 1935, vol.2, pp.108–9), indicating that, rightly or wrongly, the Great Powers identified him as the personification of trends since 1789. The decision to send Napoleon to St Helena and to keep him there, and the measures taken to enforce his captivity, confirm just how dangerous he was still thought to be. No one could know that he would die in exile in 1821 at the age of 51.

### Restoration, reaction, repression

Events in France and Europe made Stendhal's biography of Napoleon especially topical in the years immediately after his fall. The first was the repressive policy of the restoration Bourbon government in France. That policy was dictated by the so-called ***ultras***, Bourbon supporters in a Chamber of Deputies dominated by royalists 'more royalist than the king'. The *ultras,* it was said, had forgotten nothing and learned nothing since 1789. The king himself, the elderly and uninspiring Louis XVIII (r.1814–24), was moderate, had granted a liberal constitution or '**Charter**' in 1814, and hoped for peace and quiet. However, the *ultras,* mostly former émigrés led by the king's brother and heir, the bigoted Comte d'Artois (later Charles X, r.1824–30), encouraged a policy of repression, purges, reprisals and revenge against the supporters of Napoleon (now referred to as 'the usurper'). This policy was characterized by the trial and execution of Marshal Ney in 1815 (LN, p.76), a '**White Terror**' carried out under the white flag of the Bourbons at Nîmes in 1816, and the suppression of a conspiracy in favour of Napoleon's infant son (Napoleon II) at Lyons in 1817 (Bluche, 1981, pp.37–8; LN, pp.46, 174).

Stendhal – who returned briefly to France in late 1817 (and also made a trip to England) – relates in *A Life of Napoleon* the government's policy

*(LN)*
*Almost as a criticism of the 'Bourbon' government.*

of reaction: the numerous violations of the Charter, the reimposition of
censorship, the attempts to suppress and 'rubbish' Napoleon's memory.
These included the banning from Paris of Napoleon's Old Guard (p.193),
the prohibition on the tricolour flag (p.185), the removal of Napoleon's
name from the membership of the Académie française (p.195) – measures
of retaliation carried out even during the first Bourbon restoration in 1814.
In addition, there were policies aimed at the 'imminent resurrection of the
Old Regime' (p.196, and see chapters 75 to 83). 'The present government',
Stendhal wrote in *A Life of Napoleon,* 'is as tyrannical as can be' (p.120
footnote).

Reaction in France was mirrored across continental Europe by the policy
of the so-called **Holy Alliance**, the aspiration of Emperor Alexander I of
Russia but masterminded by the Austrian chancellor, Metternich. 'You see
in me', Metternich declared in 1817, 'the chief Minister of Police in
Europe. I keep an eye on everything' (quoted in Anderson, 1985, p.3).
Within and outside France, the Napoleonic era was denounced as rulers
tried to clamp down on liberal ideas, which they associated both with
the Revolution and with Napoleon, and to impose the ideology of what
they termed 'legitimacy': that is, the restoration of territories and peoples
to their former dynastic rulers. Milan, where Stendhal wrote the *Life,* was
the capital of Lombardy, hitherto 'France's most devoted ally' (LN, p.29),
now restored by the Congress of Vienna to Austrian rule. Napoleon was
still much admired in Milan. Against this background, while the
authorities in France and Europe fostered a 'black legend' of Napoleon as
'a monster of inhumanity' (p.30) and the *ultras* mocked him (in the title
of a typical publication) as the cowardly *Corsican Brigand, Nicolas
Buonaparte* (Heisler, 1969, p.90), to his admirers Napoleon's rule
appeared in retrospect a reign of enlightenment, liberation, colour, glory
and drama. 'We are bored', Stendhal commented, 'since Napoleon's
departure ... Europe seems deprived of sunlight' (1986, p.362).

## 'The prisoner of St Helena'

Another factor which moved Stendhal to write in Napoleon's defence
was his tragic fate as 'the prisoner of Saint Helena' (LN, p.103). Angered
by the denigration of Napoleon after his fall and by his banishment –
'imprisoned upon a rock' (p.100) – Stendhal was moved to write in
vindication of 'a man who, for the past four years, has been exposed to
the vengeance of all the powers on earth' (p.21). Stendhal denounced
the British as the nation chiefly responsible for Napoleon's plight in St
Helena, 'where,' he alleged, 'by indirect means and by avoiding the
odium of poison, they seek to do away with him' (p.100). Stendhal was
impressed by Napoleon's fortitude in adversity: 'his greatness of soul in
misfortune' (p.217) under the petty regime of Sir Hudson Lowe, governor
of St Helena (Figure 7.7).

*Figure 7.7   Anonymous, after Wyville,* Sir Hudson Lowe *(governor of St Helena 1816–21), 1853, engraving, 22.7 × 15.2 cm, National Portrait Gallery, London. Photo: by courtesy of the National Portrait Gallery.*

*Gauche, narrow-minded and morbidly fearful lest Napoleon escape as he had escaped from Elba in 1815, Lowe, on the orders of the Colonial Secretary, Lord Bathurst, subjected him to a mass of petty restrictions.*

*'In a few years, Lord Castlereagh [the Foreign Secretary], Lord Bathurst and you will be buried in oblivion, or if you are known, it will be for the indignities you have inflicted on me ... My body is in your power, but my spirit is free. It is as courageous as when I commanded Europe ... You are no general, you are just a pen-pushing staff officer' (Napoleon in his last interview with Lowe, 17 August 1816, after which he refused to receive him, in Aubry, 1935, vol.1, pp.227–8; trans. Lentin).*

**EXERCISE**   Napoleon used his sufferings at St Helena to enhance his reputation. Consider the brief excerpts in Anthology I, p.117: (a) 24 August 1816, (b) 21 October 1816, (c) 2 November 1816, (d) 18–19 November 1816, and (e) letter to Sir Hudson Lowe, 25 July 1817. Note briefly what points you think Napoleon replicates or adds to those made by Stendhal in chapter 40 (pp.100–1) and the last but one paragraph of chapter 87 (pp.217–18).

**DISCUSSION**   In (a) Napoleon presents himself as the harbinger and persecuted 'Messiah' of 'liberal opinions'.

In (b), while Stendhal laments that Europe 'appears to listen to those who accuse him' (p.101), Napoleon expresses confidence that his historical reputation is unassailable.

In (c), Napoleon argues that his reputation is positively enhanced by his exile and purged of its tyrannical associations.

In (d), Napoleon mirrors Stendhal's point about 'his greatness of soul in misfortune' (p.217).

In (e), Napoleon addresses a dignified and dismissive letter to Lowe. Like Stendhal, Napoleon reproaches the British government with 'injustice and persecution'. These, however, and his 'misfortune' will, he claims, enhance his reputation by lending him a 'crown of thorns'. Presenting himself as a martyr, Napoleon (through his reference to the crown of thorns) again implicitly compares his fate to that of Christ. (This letter, written in the name of his Grand Marshal of the Palace, General Bertrand, is mentioned by Stendhal in footnote 266, p.101.)

**EXERCISE**   If you have not done so already, you should now listen to Audio 3, tracks 8–12, which bring out further aspects of 'images of Napoleon'. Before listening you should refer to the AV Notes and the illustrations associated with the programme (see Illustrations Book, Plates A3.5–A3.7).

### 'To refute a slander'

A further circumstance which prompted Stendhal to write in Napoleon's defence was the appearance in 1818 of the highly critical account of him which Stendhal read with mounting indignation in June 1818. 'I am writing the history of Napoleon to refute a slander': these, as you may remember, are the opening words of chapter 1 (p.21). The 'slander' was Mme de Staël's *Reflections on the Main Events of the French Revolution*, published shortly after her death. The fourth and fifth parts of her book (excerpted in Anthology I, pp.118–21) form a critical commentary on Napoleon and his career. Staël condemned Napoleon as un-French, a

complete egoist and Machiavellian, a despot who betrayed the ideals of
the Revolution for his own selfish ends. This was no vulgar pastiche in
the style of *The Corsican Brigand,* but a serious analysis by an influential
writer and leader of opinion. As such it had correspondingly greater
weight (and a huge circulation of 60,000). As Stendhal objected, it gave
aid and comfort to Napoleon's enemies and lent credence to the 'black
legend' fostered by the *ultras*. Stendhal was infuriated by Staël's attacks:
'she insults Napoleon in the name of aristocracy and royalty', he
complained (Del Litto, 1962, p.579). Stendhal, who had stopped work on
the *Life* in January 1818, returned to it in June more determined than
ever to vindicate Napoleon's reputation (Martineau, 1950, p.175).

*Motivations for writing*

If you wish to sample the excerpts from Staël's *Reflections* in the
Anthology (also to be read in section 9) and/or the account of Staël
portrayed in Video 2, band 2 (*Women and Portraiture in Napoleonic
Europe*, to be viewed when you study Unit 9), feel free to do so now.

## Why was *A Life of Napoleon* not published in Stendhal's lifetime?

Stendhal certainly wrote with a view to publication, and one might think
that 1818 was an ideal moment to publish, with public interest in
Napoleon still intense. Why, then, did he never publish? It was probably
because (as is clear from his marginal comments and those of his friend
Vismara) he regarded the work as incomplete, and intended to make
further revisions which he never got around to.

**EXERCISE**   Can you suggest another reason why Stendhal did not publish *A Life of
Napoleon*? The first three paragraphs of chapter 79 (pp.191–2) may
prompt an answer.

**DISCUSSION**   Stendhal pours contempt on the policies of the restoration government
(he describes them as 'ridiculous' and 'absurd') inspired by the *ultras*, the
émigré nobles and priests who returned to France in 1814 and hoped to
put the clock back to before 1789. He attacks government measures
taken in breach of the Charter of 1814. He also ridicules the Catholic
faith. Publication of such outspoken attacks on government and religion,
let alone his positive appraisal of Napoleon, would have made
publication in restoration France highly unlikely.

The Bourbons appear in the book thinly disguised by initials or
pseudonyms: on p.59 Stendhal openly refers to 'the stupidity of the
Bourbons', and in chapter 30 he alludes to the possibility of their
assassination. He makes defamatory references to the king's ministers

and to men who, having abandoned Napoleon, now served the Bourbons – 'the same sycophants, who have merely changed masters' (p.163). See, for example, his description of Napoleon's two former ministers, now Louis XVIII's: the foreign minister Talleyrand – 'the corrupt man who enjoyed the king's confidence' (p.186) – and Fouché, the minister of police – 'this famous traitor' (p.44) – or his description of 'all those who have received the Legion of Honour during the past three years' as 'the most naive, stupid and mediocre people in France' (p.128 footnote). The re-establishment of censorship under a law of sedition of  November 1815 made it a criminal offence to express views favourable to Napoleon. (Stendhal refers to this on p.21 where he mentions 'the courts of summary jurisdiction'.) So he must have known that his *Life of Napoleon* stood little chance of publication in France.

Booksellers with whom he broached the possibility took fright (Stendhal, 1986, p.xxxix). Stendhal's own repeated marginal exclamations – 'careful', 'very careful' – show that he was well aware that what he was writing was dangerous. Publication anywhere could have wrecked his own career prospects. As it was, as a former servant of the empire, he was suspect to the Bourbons; he applied unsuccessfully for a position in the administration, swearing an affidavit to prove that he had held no official post during the Hundred Days (Martineau, 1950, p.15). He was unemployed and in debt, living on half-pay on a pension from the Ministry of War supplemented by a legacy from his grandfather. (He had hopes of inheriting from his father, but the latter died bankrupt in 1819.) He had moved to Milan partly because of the high cost of living in France. (After the revolution of 1830, he was to obtain a post as French consul in Trieste.)

In Milan, now restored to Austrian rule, Metternich's police and their spies were on the lookout for liberals. It appears that Stendhal was suspected by his Italian friends of being a French spy and by the Austrian authorities of supporting the *carbonari,* advocates of liberal revolution and Italian unification. In 1820–1 there were liberal uprisings in Spain, Naples, Portugal and Piedmont. Stendhal left Milan quickly in July 1821, leaving the manuscript of *A Life of Napoleon* with a friend. He never retrieved it. It was two months after the death of Napoleon.

## Stendhal and his sources

Stendhal was conscientious about consulting primary sources. He refers in his preface to the material (mostly published between 1816 and 1817) which he studied while writing the *Life*. In chapter 87 he refers to his reliance on 'the most faithful accounts' (p.217).

Yet, as we have seen, Stendhal was also conscious of the provisional nature of his book and accepted that future historians would inevitably revise the picture of Napoleon in the light of fresh evidence. 'The whole truth about Bonaparte', he insists, 'cannot possibly be known for at least a century' (p.64), and 'Fifty years hence, the history of Napoleon will have to be rewritten every year' with the publication of fresh evidence (p.20). Stendhal strove to find the best available evidence, and he combined that with the evidence of his own experience: details he had heard from others or seen for himself as an official present at court, at meetings of the Council of State, and as a participant in the wars, notably the Russian campaign of 1812. As he notes, 'we ourselves spent several years at his court' (p.217; see also pp.150, 152 and 173 for other personal testimony: 'I can personally vouch for the truth of this fact').

*Napoleon's own words, though. He should read with care!!*

Among Stendhal's sources was Napoleon himself. Stendhal quotes the *Moniteur,* the official newspaper which retailed events as dictated (and often written) by Napoleon. Stendhal frequently cites Las Cases, and had access to his records of Napoleon's conversation before the publication of the *Mémorial de Sainte Hélène* in 1823. But Stendhal was also critical of some of Napoleon's claims in Las Cases, such as the blame he placed for his failure on his own family, which Stendhal considered 'a poor excuse' (p.216). He questioned Napoleon's alleged plan to unite Europe (see Anthology I, p.116): 'this plan, if it ever existed' (p.217).

*Scrupulous with sources, or lazy?*

Another St Helena source was the Englishman William Warden, author of *Letters from St Helena* and naval surgeon aboard *HMS Northumberland,* the ship that took Napoleon into exile. Stendhal read Warden in an abridged form in the *Edinburgh Review* in December 1816, and indeed he made Warden's material the structural basis of *A Life of Napoleon.* No fewer than 27 chapters of the *Life* are based on his translations from Warden.[18] Likewise chapters 76–85 are taken verbatim from an account of the Hundred Days by another English eyewitness, Byron's friend John Cam Hobhouse. Another St Helena source used by Stendhal, which we considered earlier (Anthology I, p.115), was published by the Irish doctor O'Meara as *Napoleon in Exile or a Voice from St Helena* (1822) and in an earlier version as *Letters from the Cape of Good Hope* (1817).

---

**EXERCISE**       If you have not already read the set chapters from Stendhal's *Life of Napoleon,* you should do so now before you proceed to the next section. See p.13 for a list of the required chapters.

---

[18] Napoleon's own estimate of Warden's book was mixed: 'It has a basis of truth, but also contains a load of balls' (Martineau, 1976, p.16). At the instigation of Lord Bathurst, colonial secretary, Warden (like O'Meara) was cashiered from the navy for defending Napoleon, but was later reinstated.

# 6  Stendhal's Napoleon – 'the modern hero'

**EXERCISE**    After reading the excerpts from Stendhal's *Life of Napoleon* you should have formed a clear impression of the qualities which Stendhal attributes to Napoleon and finds so attractive. Jot down some of the qualities which Stendhal admires.

**DISCUSSION**    Probably your list includes qualities like greatness, heroism, dynamism, willpower, decisiveness, a sense of the dramatic – attributes particularly admired by the Romantics.        *STARTING POINT*

## Charisma

For Stendhal, Napoleon was a 'great man' (pp.30, 34, 61, 148, 150, 214, 215), characterized by colossal energy and dash, physical, mental and moral, as well as '*inflexible willpower*' (p.115 footnote). These heroic qualities were offset by an unheroic physique. As a young man, Stendhal writes (p.35):

> This very great spirit inhabited a pale, thin, almost puny body. The man's activity, and the strength with which, despite such a poor physique, he withstood fatigue, appeared to his army to be beyond the bounds of possibility. It was one of the main reasons for the incredible enthusiasm which he inspired in the rank and file.

Throughout his career Napoleon sped tirelessly from end to end of Europe and from one battle to another. Stendhal describes his dynamism as, again, almost superhuman (p.115):

> The speed at which he travelled, his aptitude for braving every kind of fatigue, were part of the magic of his being; and everyone, down to the most insignificant postillion, felt that he was a man above other men.

Napoleon was, to use a modern epithet, 'charismatic', an inspirational leader with flair and panache, whose mere presence charged his followers – above all, the army – with a Romantic spirit of personal devotion and reckless self-sacrifice. He inspired 'the cult of Glory; the unexpected; an absolute enthusiasm for glory which meant that a quarter of an hour afterwards one let oneself be killed with pleasure' (p.150).

## 'Genius'

All these attributes of Napoleon were linked to the concept of 'genius'. Stendhal describes him as 'an outstanding genius' (p.117), 'one of the greatest geniuses who ever lived' (p.167). Genius – the quality of the extraordinary individual – is a key concept in the transition from Enlightenment to Romanticism. The article 'Genius' by Saint-Lambert in the *Encyclopédie* defined genius as 'range of mind, power of imagination and responsiveness of soul' (Gendzier, 1967, p.118), and stressed spontaneity, immediacy, intuition and creative inspiration, an elusive quality of personal flair which transcends mere intelligence and diligence.

**EXERCISE**   Let us apply this definition to a particular passage (not part of your set reading). Stendhal is describing Napoleon's reactions when he invaded Spain in November 1808. What, according to Stendhal, are the characteristics of Napoleon's 'genius'?

> No sooner had Napoleon set foot in Spain than he found beautiful what he saw and wished to have a part of it. Nothing was more opposed to the transactions of Bayonne [where in May 1808 Napoleon had browbeaten the Spanish Bourbons into surrendering the Crown, and made his brother Joseph King of Spain]. This quick-minded and intense genius, momentarily satisfied at the time of creation, constantly perceived fresh connections between things. The new idea of each day supplanted that of the previous evening, and as he felt himself to be strong enough to overcome all obstacles, nothing was immutable to a mind before which the bounds of the possible receded as the horizon before the traveller. Napoleon has often been thought treacherous when he was merely changeable. This was the frame of mind which made him, of all European princes, the least suited to a constitutional form of government.
>
> (p.113)

**DISCUSSION**   Stendhal brings out the immediacy and spontaneity of Napoleon's reaction to Spain, his aesthetic response to its beauty, accompanied by the wish to own part of it himself, to rule it directly (rather than as a satellite-kingdom under his brother). In the third and fourth sentences Stendhal brings out Napoleon's rapidity of apprehension and soaring creative imagination, his rapidly changing perception of new possibilities and how he might accomplish them, his boundless will, self-confidence and sense of invincibility. In the last two sentences Stendhal claims that Napoleon's reputation for unreliability ('treacherous') was rather a reflection of his roaming imagination and resulting frequent changes of mind. The genius is not bound by the conventional rules to which ordinary mortals are subject.

## Military genius

Few would deny Stendhal's claim that Napoleon was a *military* genius.[19] Already by the age of 26, Stendhal writes, he could be compared with 'an Alexander, a Caesar, a Hannibal and a Frederick the Great' (p.29). Stendhal cites the 'immortal victories' of the Italian campaign against Austria 1796–7 and notes 'their miraculous quality' (p.28). Of this campaign Stendhal observes: 'No general of ancient or modern times has won so many great battles in so short a space of time, with such inadequate means and over such powerful enemies' (p.29). Likewise his victory over Russia and Austria at Austerlitz in 1805, 'probably a masterpiece of its kind', 'was to confer fresh brilliance on the emperor's military reputation, and raised him to a peak of greatness such as Europe had not seen in any sovereign since the time of Charlemagne' (p.79).

For all that, you may have noted that Stendhal barely mentions Napoleon's campaigns and battles except in passing, and never goes into detail. Though Napoleon was at war throughout his career, and war necessarily forms the background to *A Life of Napoleon,* it is not Stendhal's essential theme. Stendhal pays tribute to Napoleon's victories; he never describes them.[20] It is not, then, Napoleon the soldier who primarily interests Stendhal – he more or less takes for granted his hero's military genius – but other aspects of his character, influence and historical significance.

## Napoleon's 'fatalism'

Another side of Napoleon with a strong Romantic appeal brought out by Stendhal was his 'fatalism' (p.35). This had two meanings. On the one hand, Napoleon's long and unbroken run of success led him and others to believe in his invincibility, in 'the emperor's lucky star. The prestige of Fate was his' (p.86). On the other hand, Napoleon was an avowed fatalist, a believer in 'chance, which after all rules the world' (p.70). He professed to believe that '*it is always better to let a man fulfil his destiny, whatever it may be*' (p.42). On one battlefield in 1814 he deliberately stepped over a live shell: 'I am inclined to think', wrote Stendhal, 'that he

---

[19] Corelli Barnett's *Bonaparte* (1997) is a rare exception. Owen Connelly (1999) takes a measured view.

[20] Stendhal was present at the battles of Borodino (1812) and Bautzen (1813). In his fictitious account of the battle of Waterloo in *The Charterhouse of Parma*, he drew on his experience of Bautzen in suggesting the irrational chaos of a battle.

He nearly lost at Marengo, but for Desaix.

was putting his fate to the test' (p.171). In 1815, in reconciling himself to the prospect of exile in St Helena (he contemplated the alternative of suicide, which he had actually attempted in 1814), Napoleon made the same observation about fulfilling his destiny (see the caption to Figure 7.4, p.31).

## Administrative genius

*a good administrator*

Stendhal admired Napoleon as a remarkable administrator and legislator, who left a lasting impact on France and the territories under French control (see Figure 7.8). 'All decrees appertaining to organization ... proclaimed an outstanding genius' (p.117). 'The meetings of the Council of State were occasions for the emperor to show his brilliance' (p.130). Stendhal describes Napoleon's rule as 'the admirable French administration: an administration which ... is still missed in Belgium, Italy and the Rhineland provinces'[21] and 'something that will never be improved upon' (p.131).

The point needs stressing, since perhaps Napoleon's most enduring legacy, certainly to France and possibly to Europe, was indeed as a civilian administrator: in France the restoration of law and order and the consolidation of internal peace after ten years of revolutionary turmoil, amnesty for émigré nobles and a policy of national reconciliation and unity, the stabilizing of the currency, the regulation of church–state relations coupled with the guarantee of religious freedom, the promotion of a national educational system (see LN, chapter 21 for some of these measures). Administration was organized across the French empire and in the client-states under French control by a modern, professional salaried bureaucracy, operating according to uniform principles inherited from the Revolution and deriving from the Enlightenment. Napoleon was responsible, in other words, for the creation of a modern state structure in France and its introduction (with variants adapted to local conditions) in the annexed territories and the client-states; it was also introduced more broadly across Europe (see Figure 7.9), where the French example was followed by reforms elsewhere, notably in Prussia, Austria and even in Russia.

## The Code Napoléon

Napoleon declared in St Helena that his most lasting achievement was not his military victories but his codification of civil laws: the Civil Code of 1804 or Code Napoléon, as it was called from 1807. Stendhal, who agreed that it was 'his finest work', also underlined the paradox – 'an example unique in history' – that 'it is to her greatest military leader that

[21] Belgium, Italy and the Rhineland provinces were taken from France by the Congress of Vienna under the treaties of Paris, 1814 and 1815.

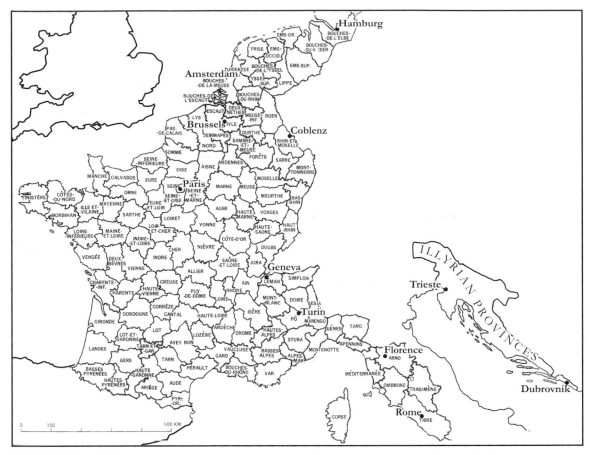

*Figure 7.8   Map showing the 130 departments of the French empire at its fullest extent, 1812,* © *Louis Bergeron,* L'épisode napoléonien: aspects intérieurs 1799–1815, *Seuil, 1972, and Michael Broers,* Europe under Napoleon 1799–1815, *Edward Arnold (Publishers) Limited, 1996.*

*The French empire at its height extended from Amsterdam and Hamburg to Rome, and included Brussels, Coblenz, Geneva, Turin, Florence, and Trieste and Dubrovnik on the Adriatic.*

*'What then were the merits of this imperial administration so missed in France, as well as by Belgium, Piedmont, the Roman States and Florence? They consisted of general rules and basic laws dictated by the soundest reasoning. All the abuses which had accumulated in the administration of every country after two or three centuries ... were completely abolished'* (LN, p.121).

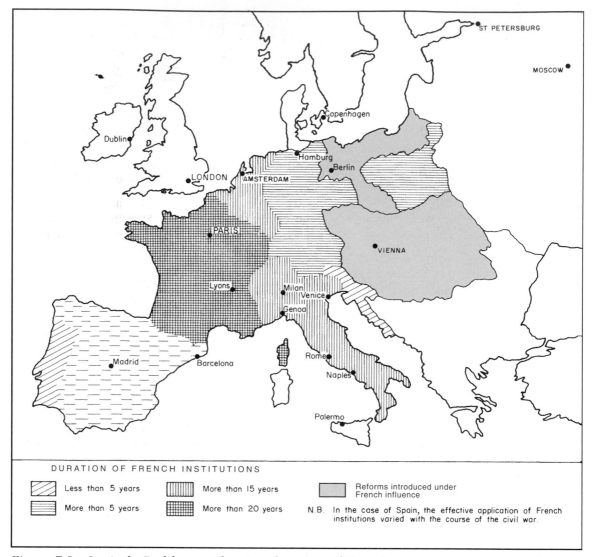

*Figure 7.9    Lucinda Rodd, map showing duration of French institutions in Europe, from N. Hampson,* The First European Revolution 1776–1815, *Thames and Hudson, 1969.*

*Much of the Code Napoléon remained in force in France and Belgium until the late twentieth century and in the Rhineland until the late nineteenth century. It influenced the laws of Holland, Germany, Switzerland, Italy, Poland and Illyria (present-day Croatia).*

*'I have framed and carried into effect a code of laws that will bear my name to the most distant posterity' (Napoleon, 1817, in Anthology I, p.115).*

France owes the ending of the confusion and contradictions in the labyrinth of laws by which she was governed' (p.57). The drafting of a uniform civil code had been an aim of the Enlightenment and was demanded by the deputies to the Estates-General in 1789. Work on it began during the Revolution, but it was Napoleon who appointed a legislative commission of the Council of State to integrate French law and to codify the achievements of the Revolution. The Code Napoléon confirmed the abolition of feudal privilege, laying down equality before the law, freedom of religion and civil marriage. It also confirmed the title of purchasers of land confiscated from the Church and nobility. These new property owners were among the keenest supporters of the regime.

Of the commission's 102 sessions, Napoleon himself chaired 57. He intervened frequently, dominating the discussion. Stendhal describes his interventions as 'astounding' (p.130). Napoleon propelled some parts of the Civil Code in a counter-revolutionary direction, particularly the sections on paternal authority, which strengthened the rights of the male head of the family over his wife and children. A wife was legally bound to obey her husband, and could enter into no significant legal transaction without his consent. Her status was that of a minor. In the matter of divorce, introduced during the Revolution in 1792, Napoleon also went back on the principle of the equality of man and wife and reduced the grounds of divorce from seven to three. A husband could divorce his wife (and even have her imprisoned) for adultery; a wife had no redress against her husband's adultery unless he installed his mistress in the matrimonial home. On the other hand, Napoleon retained divorce by mutual consent, mainly because he thought this would facilitate his contemplated divorce from Josephine. (In general, divorce was rare and provision for divorce was repealed in 1816. It was not reintroduced until 1880.)[22]

Having in 1799 confirmed the abolition of slavery in France's overseas colonies proclaimed by the Convention in 1794, Napoleon reimposed it in 1803, telling the Council of State:

> I am for the whites, because I am white. I have no other reason, and it is a good reason. How could they [the Convention] grant

[22] In fairness, it should be pointed out that the legal status of women in early nineteenth-century Britain was no better. Note Stendhal's approval of Napoleon's contributions on matrimonial law as 'some of the wisest provisions in the Civil Code' (p.131).

freedom to Africans, to utterly uncivilised men who did not even know what a colony was, what France was?[23]

(Herold, 1955, p.189)

## Napoleon's 'enlightened absolutism'

The Civil Code, the constitutions of 1799, 1802 and 1804, and the French administrative and judicial system were extended across the French empire and imposed with local modifications in the client-states. This suggests Napoleon's essentially Enlightenment view of the basic uniformity of European peoples and the applicability throughout Europe of French laws and institutions. In 1805 he told his Council of State:

> The annexed territories must be just like France, and if you went on annexing everything as far as Gibraltar and Kamchatka, the laws of France would have to spread there too.

(Herold, 1955, p.72; see also Anthology I, pp.109–10)

In recruiting men to serve in the army and administration, Napoleon encouraged meritocracy. He professed the principle, lying at the heart of the Revolution, of 'a career open to all talents, without distinctions of birth' (Herold, 1955, p.73). Stendhal commends his encouragement of merit through the Legion of Honour (p.128):

> The most insignificant chemist's apprentice working in his master's back-room was stirred by the thought that should he make some great discovery, he would receive the Cross of the Legion of Honour, and be made a count.

The spirit of Napoleon's rule, however, was of enlightenment 'from above'. Already in the 1790s, as Michael Broers argues of revolutionary France and its satellites, 'those in authority began to regard those they governed less as fellow-citizens than as *les administrés,* "the administered"' (Broers, 1996, p.11). The excesses of the Revolution – and Napoleon had personally witnessed the sack of the Tuileries in 1792 – left him with a deep and lasting distaste for the *sans-culottes,* public unrest, democratic politics and factional strife. '[T]he revolutionary times are over,' he declared in 1805, 'and ... there is but one single party in

---

[23] In 1802 Napoleon sent an expedition to retake the Caribbean island of Santo Domingo (Haiti), which declared its independence under the black revolutionary leader, Toussaint L'Ouverture. L'Ouverture died in captivity in France in 1803. The prison governor refused him medical care, 'since the anatomy of Negroes in no way resembles that of Europeans' (Sibalis, 2001, p.91). Stendhal compares Napoleon's methods with 'the treachery and cruelty of Philip II' of Spain (p.60). In 1817 Napoleon told Gourgaud that his policy on slavery, Santo Domingo and Toussaint L'Ouverture was 'the greatest mistake I ever made in my administration' (Herold, 1955, p.189).

France' (Anthology I, p.107). In his rule, which he saw as being in the interests of the nation as a whole, he displayed a marked preference for law and order, social stability, and authoritarian rule from Paris by a powerful, centralized executive, overseeing practical reform and reaching out to the departments of the empire through a cadre of hand-picked prefects personally responsible to him. These predilections – apolitical, pragmatic, technocratic, meritocratic – characterize Napoleon's administration.

As already suggested, Napoleon set little store by the free institutions and representative assemblies introduced under the Revolution. These he regarded as time-wasting, obstructive and divisive. He preferred sound administration by an elite of trained professionals – bureaucrats, soldiers, judges, civil engineers (for the building of roads and other public works) – all men appointed by him. Some historians trace his ideas and mode of government to the concept of the 'well ordered police-state' favoured in the eighteenth century by 'enlightened despots' such as Frederick the Great of Prussia, Catherine the Great of Russia and Joseph II of Austria. Stendhal puts into his mouth the following sentiments (p.132):

> The despot said to his subjects: 'Cross your arms, my prefects will take care of everything for you. As the price of such sweet repose, I only ask for your children and money [that is, recruits and taxes]'.

# 7   'The wholly Roman character of Napoleon'

Stendhal's 'modern hero' stood four-square in another Enlightenment tradition: the heritage of the classics, which, as we saw in Unit 6, also permeated the revolutionary period. The historian Constantin-François Chasseboeuf, Comte de Volney (1757–1820) suggested that during the Revolution enthusiasm for the cult of antiquity displaced zeal for Christianity: men turned to Livy for their Bible, to Plutarch for their 'Lives of Saints and Martyrs' (Parker, 1937, pp.2–3). Certainly Napoleon was steeped in classical history. You may remember his admiration for Alexander the Great and his allusion to Plutarch's life of Themistocles in his appeal to the Prince Regent (Figure 7.3, p.29).

## Republican hero in the Roman mode

Stendhal too, like most of his contemporaries, was brought up on the classics. His generation was inspired by examples from republican history, in particular Plutarch's *Lives of the Greeks and Romans* and Livy's *History of Rome*. Stendhal refers to Livy and Plutarch respectively when describing Napoleon at the beginning and end of his career (pp.31 footnote, 217). He compares Napoleon to the military heroes of the ancient world as well as of recent history: 'no general of ancient or modern times' could vie with him (p.29). Even as a schoolboy, 'he was known ... by his passion for imitating the manner, and even the language, of the great men of antiquity' (p.23).

Stendhal goes so far as to write of 'the wholly Roman character of Napoleon' (p.148 footnote), and describes him as 'imbued with Roman ideas' (p.53). These included such Roman characteristics as 'ambition and love of country' and 'the hope of leaving a great name to posterity' (p.43).

From his references to Livy, it is clear that Stendhal saw the young Napoleon as a modern counterpart to the heroic Roman generals of the republic celebrated by Livy (for example, Publius Cornelius Scipio, who defeated Hannibal in the second century BCE). Of the Italian campaign of 1796–7 Stendhal says that Napoleon 'restored this most beautiful part of the Roman empire to life, and in a trice appeared to have also restored its ancient virtues' (p.29). Of his exile at St Helena, referring to his 'simplicity and greatness of soul' (p.67), Stendhal suggests that Napoleon's conduct harked back to classical examples of greatness: 'it is perhaps this which puts us most in mind of Plutarch's heroes' (p.217). In general, for Stendhal, 'this man's whole life is a paean in praise of greatness of soul' (p.43). To the ancients, 'greatness of soul' was the characteristic of the hero.

For Stendhal, the most Roman and most admirable part of Napoleon's career was as a young general of the republic 1796–9 and as First Consul 1799–1804. As liberator of northern Italy, Napoleon brought about 'those victories of a young republic over an ancient despotism' (that is, Habsburg rule) and inaugurated 'a great and wonderful era for Europe' (pp.28–9). Napoleon as First Consul was 'that intrepid mind' (p.58). His early measures were 'noble, wise and beneficial' (p.54).

Early admirers (including Mme de Staël, though she soon changed her mind) compared Napoleon as First Consul to Lucius Junius Brutus, also a consul (Rome's first) and austere republican hero (sixth century BCE), famed for expelling the ancient kings of Rome. There was even said to be a physical resemblance between Napoleon and this Brutus (whose descendant, Marcus Junius Brutus, was likewise celebrated as the man who killed Julius Caesar in 44 BCE to save the republic from Caesar's ambition to become king). Ancient busts of both Brutuses were taken from Rome ('liberated' by republican France in 1798), and a bust of Lucius Junius Brutus was placed in the Tuileries palace, where Napoleon took up residence. A bust of George Washington, first President of the United States under its republican constitution, also graced the Tuileries when Napoleon commemorated Washington's death in 1799.

## Napoleon as classical tyrant

Yet as his tale unfolds, Stendhal repeatedly states that Napoleon was or became 'a tyrant' or 'despot', albeit 'a despot who was at the same time a man of genius' (p.79). There was never any denying that genius: 'Whoever says tyrant says superior mind' (p.214). Nonetheless Stendhal insists that Napoleon remained a tyrant, 'a nineteenth-century tyrant' (p.214), suggesting comparisons with tyrants of previous ages. 'Tyrant' was a striking word to use, one with strong negative classical and revolutionary resonances. (Think of the first verse of the *Marseillaise* – see Anthology I, p.100.)

## Napoleon's 'shaky republicanism': the First Consul

In chapter 7 Stendhal argues that as early as 1797 Napoleon's 'republicanism was already very shaky' (p.33). By 1799 'it was obvious that either he or the Bourbons were going to ascend the throne' (p.45). Napoleon's seizure of power in the *coup d'état* of 18th Brumaire 1799 was based on his conviction that 'I am better for France than the Bourbons' (p.45). A new constitution, drawn up by Sieyès (known as 'the Constitution of the Year VIII' – LN, p.51), was approved by plebiscite and promulgated by a special senatorial edict or *senatus-consultum*.[24] As First Consul, in whom real power was vested, Napoleon had two lesser colleagues, also consuls. There was an ambiguity about the title of First Consul. The consulship was an office drawn from republican Rome, where two consuls served annually with equal authority: there was no 'first' consul in ancient Rome.

Under the constitution of 1799 Napoleon was to be First Consul for ten years. Sieyès aimed to counter an over-powerful executive under Napoleon not only through the two lesser consuls, but also by dividing legislative functions between various organs and through a system of institutional checks and balances (see LN, pp.50–1, for details). Napoleon, however, gradually dismantled the constitution of 1799. He purged the Tribunat in 1802 and abolished it in 1807 by a *senatus-consultum* (LN, pp.58–9). The Senate, which consisted of his own appointees, simply ratified his decisions. Stendhal roundly describes Napoleon's consulship as 'a military despotism' (p.51).

Yet Stendhal also saw it as a necessary despotism: 'without this military despotism, France would have had, in 1800, the events of 1814 [a Bourbon counter-revolution] or else the Terror' (p.51). Here again Stendhal endorses Napoleon's own claim that he came as a liberator in 1799 to save France from civil war and to preserve the gains of the

[24] By arranging the promulgation of a *senatus-consultum* Napoleon avoided referring a matter to the Tribunat or the Legislative Body, where it might have been opposed or at least criticized. He frequently resorted to *senatus-consulta*.

Revolution, and that, in Napoleon's words, 'dictatorship was absolutely necessary' (Anthology I, p.114). Yet Stendhal's attitude to that dictatorship was ambivalent. For him, however 'necessary', dictatorship was clearly objectionable in itself. The main inspiration behind the Revolution, after all, had been the hope of liberation from tyranny.

Napoleon consolidated and massively extended his hold on power in 1802, when, in Stendhal's words, 'a servile Senate and a heedless people made him consul for life with power to designate his successor' (p.62) (see Figure 7.10). Again a *senatus-consultum* announced the result of a plebiscite. Stendhal describes the First Consul as 'the dictator' (p.54), adding that 'the constitution which he gave to France was calculated ... to bring a fine country back to an absolute monarchy' (p.54). Let us consider the truth of this charge.

*Figure 7.10    Medal in Roman style commemorating the peace of Amiens with England, 1802, from André Maurois,* Napoleon: A Pictorial Biography, *London, Thames and Hudson, 1963.*

*The obverse shows Napoleon as First Consul wearing a wreath of victory. Note what is not shown. The slogan 'Liberty, Equality, Fraternity' had been phased out in 1801. There is no reference to the French Republic. The date is given according to both the Gregorian calendar and the revolutionary calendar (which Napoleon abolished in 1806). In 1803 it was decreed that all coins would carry Napoleon's effigy. Napoleon became consul for life in May 1802, two months after the peace of Amiens. Thus the portrait may suggest Caesar, dictator for life, rather than the exemplary republican Brutus.*

**EXERCISE**        Now read Napoleon's comments to Joseph Bonaparte on political opposition, 1803 (Anthology I, p.106). How far do they bear out Stendhal's description of Napoleon as 'the dictator'?

**DISCUSSION**  Napoleon, hostile to the notion of parliamentary opposition on the English model (since in his view 'its only result is to diminish the prestige of authority in the eyes of the people') and clearly determined to 'silence' his extra-parliamentary critics, speaks of the need for 'absolute unity of power': that is, the concentration of power in his own hands. This certainly seems to bear out Stendhal's claim.

## Napoleon's 'crimes'

You may recall Napoleon's claim that his rise to power was 'unaccompanied by any crime' (Anthology I, p.115). If this refers to the coup of 18th Brumaire, it is perhaps justified, though Stendhal sometimes seems to see the coup itself as a crime against freedom. See his praise of the deputy Bigonnet, who opposed it: 'This brave deputy should have killed Bonaparte' (p.49).

But there were other acts which Napoleon's critics, then and later, did not hesitate to denounce as 'crimes' (p.38). Among such critics were Mme de Staël and what Stendhal disparagingly calls 'bourgeois historians' (p.38). He devotes several chapters to considering their accusations, notably:

- atrocities committed during the Egyptian campaign, 1798–9 (chapters 11–13);
- the suspicious death in captivity of General Pichegru and the British agent Captain Wright, both involved in the royalist Cadoudal conspiracy against Napoleon, and Napoleon's banishment to Guyana of a potential rival, the republican general Moreau, in 1804 (chapters 24–7);
- the kidnapping, summary trial and execution by firing squad in 1804 of the 32-year-old Duke d'Enghien, a member of the house of Bourbon (p.64 and chapters 27–9). For many of Napoleon's critics in France and abroad, d'Enghien's murder was a turning-point in Napoleon's career. 'He crossed the Rubicon of crime,' wrote Staël (Anthology I, p.119).

If you wish to explore them further, feel free to consider Stendhal's detailed discussion of these charges. They are, after all, central to any interpretation of Napoleon's character and the nature of his regime. Stendhal comes out largely on Napoleon's side on the grounds that 'the primary law for him was to survive' (p.53).

*in the first year of his Consulate. (p.53)*

## 'Napoleon the Great': the imperial cult

As Napoleon consolidated and extended his power, he significantly dropped much republican symbolism. Unlike all constitutions since the

Revolution, the constitutions of 1799, 1802 and 1804 were not preceded by the Declaration of the Rights of Man and Citizen of 1789. While Napoleon retained the tricolour flag, he added atop the flagpole the imperial eagle (the standard of the Roman legions, under Napoleon the regimental insignia of the French army). He continued to commemorate the fall of the Bastille on 14 July, but he discontinued the other revolutionary festivals, and – except very occasionally (see LN, p.80) and during the Hundred Days – the playing of the *Marseillaise* (Lyons, 1994, pp.138–9; Chandler, 1999, p.273). With its summons to rise up against 'tyranny', Napoleon presumably thought the revolutionary anthem too close to the knuckle.

In 1804 Napoleon achieved what Stendhal called 'the last and greatest object of his ambition' (p.64) by making himself hereditary Emperor of the French, with a civil list (personal allowance) equal to that of Louis XVI and powers far exceeding those of Louis XIV (1661–1715), the most absolute of French monarchs, in the extent of his ability to tax, control and conscript manpower. The title 'emperor' recalled imperial Roman rule and the rule of Charlemagne (768–814 CE) over the Holy Roman Empire (then consisting of Germany and most of western Europe). In *The Distribution of the Eagle Standards* (Illustrations Book, Plate 9.30), David commemorated the ceremony in 1804 when, as newly crowned emperor, Napoleon received from his generals an oath of *personal* allegiance. In 1807 Napoleon formally abolished the title of the state established by the Revolution in 1792 – the French Republic. The word 'subject' displaced the egalitarian 'citizen' (Bluche, 1981, p.27). Republican imagery was replaced by the cult of Napoleon himself. The republican cap of liberty, the lictor's axe and *fasces,* the female figure symbolizing the republic, were replaced by Napoleon in the style of a victorious Roman general, suggesting Julius Caesar or the Emperor Trajan (see Figures 7.11 and 7.12). Annual celebrations commemorated his birthday (the feast of St Napoleon), his coming to power on the 18th Brumaire, his coronation and the anniversaries of his victories at Austerlitz and Jena. These public celebrations, increasingly military in character, were comparable to Roman triumphs. Individual triumphs were celebrated in special ceremonies such as the placing of the sword of Frederick the Great in the Invalides in 1807 (LN, p.59) and the conclusion of the Treaty of Tilsit with Russia in 1807, when Napoleon assumed the title 'Napoleon the Great'.

## Napoleon's *crownomania*

Napoleon made his brothers Joseph, Louis and Jérôme kings respectively of Spain, Holland and Westphalia, his brother-in-law, Joachim Murat, King of Naples, and his step-son, Eugène Beauharnais, viceroy of the kingdom of Italy. He consorted with the traditional crowned heads of Europe (see Figure 7.13). In 1809 he divorced his first wife Josephine, who had failed to bear him a child, and married Marie-Louise, daughter

*Figure 7.11   A.E. Fragonard,* Napoleon enters Berlin after the victory of Jena in October 1806, *1813, Manufacture nationale de Sèvres archives, Sèvres. Photo: © RMN/Bulloz.*

*The city keys are surrendered by the governor, Prince von Hatzfeld (kneeling). Shortly before, Hatzfeld had communicated the position of the French forces to the King of Prussia. Napoleon was dissuaded from executing him by the pleas of Princess von Hatzfeld (on right). Napoleon's triumphal entry and his clemency are here depicted in imperial Roman style suggesting the* **bas-reliefs** *of Trajan's column (similar bas-reliefs were designed for the Vendôme column in Paris). The opera* The Triumph of Trajan, *written at Napoleon's suggestion by the composer Jean-François Lesueur, was performed in Paris in 1807. (This illustration is also variously said to represent Napoleon's entry into Ulm, October 1805, or Vienna, November 1805.)*

of the Austrian emperor, who gave him the wished-for son and heir in 1810.[25] Stendhal comments: 'He was tickled by the idea that he, a lieutenant of artillery, had succeeded in marrying' an Austrian princess (p.140). Napoleon, he says, was consumed by what Stendhal calls '*crownomania*' (p.118) and 'the vain pomp and ceremony of a court' (p.140). He quotes Napoleon: 'I found a crown in the gutter. I wiped away the mud which covered it and placed it on my head' (p.69).

For Stendhal, rationalist, utilitarian and republican, Napoleon's *crownomania* revealed a 'weakness in his character' (p.140). Monarchy held no attractions for Stendhal. His references to its mystique and trappings are contemptuous. 'Napoleon', he says, 'saw a crown before

[25] The so-called Napoleon II left France for Austria with his mother in 1814 on his father's first abdication. He died of tuberculosis in 1832.

*Figure 7.12    Antoine-Denis Chaudet (after),* Napoleon, *c.1808, bronze, 59 x 31 x 29 cm, Louvre, Paris. Photo: © RMN/R.G. Ojeda.*

*This bronze bust of Napoleon in Roman style was moulded from bronze left over from the bas-reliefs on the Vendôme column. An earlier prototype by Chaudet – a plaster model of Napoleon as First Consul made in 1799 – became the model for a mass-produced official bust. Stendhal included Chaudet among the producers of 'the least bad portraits' of Napoleon (p.35). Chaudet also produced a huge bronze statue of Napoleon in Roman style. The statue of the Republic in the place Vendôme was replaced by the Colonne de la Grande Armée, later called the Vendôme column, modelled on Trajan's column in Rome, and surmounted in 1810 by Chaudet's statue of Napoleon (Agulhon, 1981, pp.34–6). The statue was pulled down in 1814 (see LN, p.176).*

*Figure 7.13 Anonymous,* Meeting of the Sovereigns Accompanying the Emperor to the Ball *(given by the city of Paris, 4 December 1809), Musée Carnavalet, Paris. Photo: © RMN/ Bulloz.*

*From left to right: Joachim, King of Naples; Frederick-Augustus, King of Saxony-Poland; Jérôme Bonaparte, King of Westphalia; Frederick, King of Württemberg; Louis Bonaparte, King of Holland; Napoleon and Josephine, whom he divorced nine days later. Print after anonymous contemporary sketch. Note the imperial crown and eagle above the mantelpiece.*

*'In 1808, ... the changes which eight years of unhindered arrogance and* crownomania *had effected in Napoleon's genius ...' (LN, p.118).*

his eyes and let himself be dazzled by the splendour of that out-of-date bauble ... his sole ambition was to found a dynasty of kings' (p.54). Napoleon's coronation he describes as 'that absurd ceremony' (p.79), the name of emperor as 'an empty title' (p.62). Behind this lies a deeper criticism of Napoleon: 'He attained the height of folly by forgetting his main qualification, that of being a son of the Revolution' (p.140), which had abolished the monarchy in 1792.

You may remember from Unit 6 that titles of nobility were abolished in France in 1790. After 1800 émigré nobles returned to France under the amnesty offered by Napoleon. In 1808 Napoleon established his own imperial nobility and created the titles of prince and duke, as well as

count, baron and knight (*chevalier*) of the empire. All members of the
Legion of Honour (created in 1802, see LN, p.128) were knights.
Napoleon granted the wealthiest of the imperial nobles hereditary titles
and territorial estates. Nearly three-fifths of his imperial nobility were
military men, and over one-fifth were members of the Old Regime
nobility (Wolloch, 2001, pp.71–2). Stendhal was scathing about
Napoleon's new nobility and the imperial court (see chapter 52).

## Napoleon and the Church: Concordat and *Imperial Catechism*

Evidence of Napoleon's religious beliefs is conflicting. Records of his
private remarks range from scepticism or atheism to deism, and a sense
of God deriving, as with Rousseau, from feelings rather than reason
(Herold, 1955, pp.28–34). What is certain is his patronage of the Catholic
Church in France, which he saw as a vital instrument of social control
and a common focus of national loyalty: 'In religion', as he told the
Council of State in 1806, 'I do not see the mystery of the Incarnation but
the mystery of the social order' (Herold, 1955, p.105).

In 1801 Napoleon concluded, and in 1802 he published, a **Concordat** or
agreement with Pope Pius VII. While guaranteeing freedom of religion
for the half-million French Protestants and 50,000 Jews[26] and regulating
their organization as religious minorities, Napoleon declared Roman
Catholicism to be 'the religion of the vast majority of French citizens'
(Ellis, 1997, p.62). He placed the Catholic Church in France under close
state regulations drawn up by himself. The Pope for his part recognized
the Napoleonic regime, accepted as final the sale of church lands
effected during the Revolution, and agreed to approve as archbishops
and bishops Napoleon's nominees, who in turn appointed the parish
priests. All members of the clergy now received state salaries and swore
an oath of loyalty to Napoleon.

Stendhal emphasizes that Napoleon 'was praised for having restored
peace to the Church by means of his Concordat', but comments: 'This
was a great mistake, which will delay by a century the emancipation of
France. He should have been satisfied with putting an end to all
persecution' (p.56). We know that Stendhal was an anticlerical and
sceptic for whom religious belief was a matter of personal conviction that
should be left to the individual. In the spirit of the Enlightenment, he
favoured religious toleration and freedom of belief and practice, and
preferred the separation of church and state as decreed by the
Directorate in 1795.

---

[26] Napoleon's legislation on the Jews, following his summoning of a consultative
representative 'Grand Sanhedrin' at Paris in 1807, aimed at their assimilation into
French society on a footing of religious toleration and civic equality.

**EXERCISE**    Now read the extract from the *Imperial Catechism*, drawn up by Napoleon in 1806 for use in all Catholic churches in France (Anthology I, pp.107–8). What were the advantages to Napoleon of the Concordat and catechism?

**DISCUSSION**    Through his Concordat and by introducing the *Imperial Catechism*, Napoleon harnessed the Church as a powerful organization to reconcile and unite under his rule the majority of French people. Church and catechism were further instruments of control, enjoining personal allegiance and obedience to Napoleon as a solemn religious duty:

- 'Military service' and 'tributes' [i.e. taxes] are specifically listed among these duties.

- Having crowned himself as emperor in the Pope's presence in the cathedral of Notre Dame, Napoleon 'has become the Lord's anointed': in the eyes of the faithful, he rules by divine right.

- 'Eternal damnation' is threatened to 'those who may fail in their duty toward our Emperor'.

The Concordat also enabled Napoleon to outflank the Count of Provence (the future Louis XVIII), émigré brother of the executed Louis XVI and Bourbon claimant to the throne. With the Pope's public sanction, Napoleon now replaced the Bourbons as France's legitimate ruler, a duly consecrated sovereign and object of the prayers of his 'subjects'.

The *Imperial Catechism* is clear evidence of Napoleon's move away from republicanism to hereditary monarchy (his *'crownomania'*, in Stendhal's view).

## Hubris: Napoleon and the Caesars

*[handwritten margin note: part of Iaa Kershaw's 2 part book on 'Hitler']*

The ancients conceived of a tyrant as one who, wielding absolute power, is finally brought down by his own vices and by hubris, or overweening pride. Examples include Alexander the Great and Julius Caesar, both of whom Stendhal mentions in the same breath as Napoleon. Stendhal describes Napoleon as 'by his talents the finest man to have appeared since Caesar' (p.217).

Napoleon too compared himself to Alexander, as we have seen, and to Julius Caesar, the Emperor Trajan and also the Emperor Diocletian. In 1804, preparing to invade England, he told Josephine, 'I intend the wife of the modern Caesar to be crowned at Westminster' (Barnett, 1997, p.99). In 1809, in conversation with the sculptor Canova, who was modelling a statue of him, he enthused on the greatness of the Romans and exclaimed: 'But Caesar! Ah, Caesar! That was the great man!' (Geyl, 1965, p.352). In 1809 he annexed Rome itself and in 1810 proclaimed it 'the second city of the Empire' (Ellis, 1997, p.86); in 1811 he proclaimed his new-born son and heir 'the king of Rome'. In the letter in which Napoleon informed Fouché of the attempt to assassinate him in 1809, he states that his would-be assassin 'didn't seem to understand that Brutus was a murderer' (Anthology I, p.110). Napoleon's matter-of-fact dismissal of Brutus, the hero of republican tradition to whom wishful thinkers had compared him under the consulate, confirms his hostility to republican ideology noted earlier. He withdrew Voltaire's tragedy, *The Death of Caesar* (1733), from the repertoire of the Comédie Française (Holtman, 1950, p.147) and invited Goethe to rewrite it to show that Brutus was wrong to murder Caesar! (Gooch, 1931, p.175).

Stendhal may also have in mind the history of the early Roman empire, described in sombre tones by the historian Tacitus. Tacitus, another classical author with republican sympathies, was much invoked during the Enlightenment and revolutionary period, and was a particular bugbear of Napoleon for his hostile portrayal of the early Caesars: Tiberius, Caligula and Nero. Tacitus depicts Tiberius, for example, as habitually suspicious. Stendhal makes a similar comment about Napoleon: 'The despot was mistrustful' (p.138). On the day of his marriage to Marie-Louise, Stendhal says, 'he was as gloomy as Nero' (p.86). Stendhal was certainly thinking of parallels between Napoleon and the early Roman emperors, whose overthrow was commonly engineered by a palace coup of the emperor's personal bodyguard, the praetorian guards, when he wrote: 'He [Napoleon] 'saw that ... a conspiracy of the praetorian guards could cast him down from the throne to death' (p.137).

For Stendhal, then, Napoleon was 'a man endowed with amazing abilities and a dangerous ambition' (p.217), who, first in France, then across Europe, raised himself to a position of supreme and absolute power comparable to that of the Roman emperors. Moreover, he rose to power 'with a character that was already formed and inflexible' at the age of 26 (p.137). Circumstances – an unbroken run of success – brought out his innate qualities, good and bad, and turned him into a tyrant. 'Napoleon was not used to opposition,' Stendhal writes. 'His was a nature ruined by despotism and by an unheard-of series of successes' (p.92). Yet he was no mere victim of circumstances: events brought out but did not engender his basic defect, his hubris, 'that fatal blindness which little by little turned him into a common despot' (p.64 footnote). At one point Stendhal suggests that Napoleon's independent-minded brother Lucien might have dissuaded him from 'giving in' to his fatal weakness (p.64 footnote). Elsewhere, however, Stendhal insists that the flaw was inherent in Napoleon's character and that it was ineradicable: 'I have no doubt that the man would have carried the day, and that in the long run the despot would have appeared' (p.53). This same fatal defect served to bring him down. By the time he intervened in Spain in 1808, hubris had undermined his judgement and he began to overreach himself.[27] Stendhal writes of 'the changes which eight years of unhindered arrogance and *crownomania* had effected in Napoleon's genius' (p.118). You may have heard a saying of the nineteenth-century historian Lord Acton (1834–1902): 'Power tends to corrupt and absolute power corrupts absolutely.' That, in a nutshell, was Stendhal's view of Napoleon.

**EXERCISE**   If you have not already viewed Video 2, band 1, *Goya*, and consulted the AV Notes, you should do so now. The programme shows how Goya expressed through his art some of the experiences and reactions caused by Napoleon's invasion of Spain. (It also tracks the way in which Goya's Romantic sensibility evolved in a climate of disappointed hopes for Spanish Enlightenment.)

# 8   Emperor into tyrant

## 'Transition'

Stendhal sums up this process of corruption in Napoleon in a pivotal chapter 43 (pp.115–16), significantly entitled 'Transition'.

**EXERCISE**   Reread chapter 43 and briefly give examples of Stendhal's account of the deterioration in Napoleon's character by 1808.

**DISCUSSION**

- Napoleon swallowed flattery and it went to his head: 'He believed that nothing was personally impossible for him.'
- 'He could no longer stand contradiction' and considered himself infallible.
- He rejected independent-minded advisers in favour of yes-men.

Where you might have expected Stendhal to say that Napoleon grew accustomed to his good fortune and began to take it for granted, he makes the opposite and more subtle observation that 'he made the mistake of being too surprised by his success' and, in Stendhal's view,

[27] As Napoleon later admitted, the Peninsular War (1808–14) was among his biggest mistakes. It proved what he called a 'Spanish ulcer', which cost an estimated 240,000 casualties (100 lives a day), huge financial strains and economic dislocation.

held 'the kings, his colleagues' in too high esteem. Although cynical and suspicious, he was not cynical and suspicious enough. Stendhal goes on to argue that Napoleon supposed his fellow monarchs to be men of their word, and after defeating them, he spared them. But they bided their time and helped to destroy him.

In chapter 45 (p.118) Stendhal makes a striking assertion about Napoleon at the time of the invasion of Russia in 1812:

> Thirteen and a half years of success turned Alexander the Great into a kind of madman. Good fortune of exactly the same duration produced the same madness in Napoleon.

---

**EXERCISE**   Is 'madness' a plausible verdict on Napoleon by 1812? Read the extract from Fouché's memoirs (Anthology I, p.113) and assess how far it corroborates Stendhal's conclusion.

---

**DISCUSSION**   Fouché's account of Napoleon on the eve of the Russian campaign seems indeed to corroborate Stendhal's conclusion that Napoleon had become a megalomaniac, that 'he believed that nothing was personally impossible for him' and that 'he could no longer stand contradiction' (LN, p.116). Fouché reports Napoleon as intent on the conquest of Russia as a prelude to uniting Europe under French domination. According to Fouché, Napoleon presented himself as impelled by the course of events and his 'destiny' towards 'the dictatorship of the world', contemptuous of the difficulties and apparently unhinged.

*Comes from same N. quote!*

*Bound to Corroborate him!*

---

Fouché's memoirs should be approached with caution. Napoleon's minister of police, Fouché was a careerist and turncoat known to be intriguing with the Bourbons, who in 1814 went over to them, then switched back to Napoleon during the Hundred Days, and then back again to the Bourbons. (Napoleon regretted that he had not had him shot after Waterloo.) Stendhal describes Fouché as 'this famous traitor' (p.44). Fouché's aim in this excerpt was plainly to show that by 1812 Napoleon had lost touch with reality and thus to justify his (Fouché's) abandonment of him.

However, while Fouché's motives in writing should put us on our guard, they do not necessarily invalidate the reliability of his account. Napoleon himself asserted at St Helena his ultimate intention of bringing about a united Europe under French tutelage (see his conversation with Las Cases, 24 August 1816, in Anthology I, p.116). If we are to believe it, this document seems to corroborate Fouché's account.

Whatever conclusions you reach about Napoleon's state of mind and his ultimate intentions with regard to Europe, this exercise should serve to emphasize the need to consider sources critically.

While classifying Napoleon as a 'tyrant', Stendhal does not suggest that he was savage or vengeful (see chapter 30). 'Although violent and unrestrained in his fits of temper' (see pp.126, 161 footnote) – another aspect of a tyrant – 'he was neither cruel nor vindictive' (p.132). Napoleon agreed that his temper, sometimes simulated, was fearsome. In another conversation with Las Cases, he admits to a reputation for 'my tyrant's skin ... my murderousness and ferocity' (Anthology I, p.117).

## Napoleon – an 'ever mediocre political genius'

In addition to the underlying hubris, the 'arrogance and *crownomania*' (p.118) which Stendhal sees as the long-term cause of his fall, Napoleon revealed other defects of character and judgement. Stendhal argues that, far from being a deep-dyed villain, one whom 'the English and Madame de Staël present as Machiavellianism personified' (p.164), Napoleon was at crucial moments fatally soft-hearted, sentimental, full of illusion and thoroughly misguided. Stendhal makes the remarkable and unexpected assertion that Napoleon's 'greatest mistakes' came from 'a heart that was too trusting and too tender towards the interests of humanity' (p.30). This was 'a noble error of a kind that rightly confounds his detractors' (p.82).

'It is not given to one human being to have all the talents at once, and he was too superb a general to be any good as a politician' (p.53). In Stendhal's opinion, for all his military and administrative genius, Napoleon lacked political judgement. 'He had the warm heart of a soldier, but a poor head for politics' (p.91) and made 'political mistakes' (p.57). In general, Stendhal paradoxically claims, 'he was unsuited to politics' (p.82) and was 'mediocre as a monarch' (p.171). YES! And ....

Napoleon frequently professed his desire for peace. Stendhal agrees that he 'sought sincerely to restore peace to the world' (p.30), adding paradoxically: 'this was doubtless a mistake.' In Stendhal's view, Napoleon would have served his interests better had he been more ruthless towards his enemies when he had them at his mercy: 'a defeated ruler should never be spared' (p.153). Far from Machiavellian, Napoleon was politically naive:

- After smashing Austria and Prussia at Austerlitz and Jena, he should have replaced their rulers with his own nominees. By leaving the Hohenzollern and Habsburg monarchs in power, says Stendhal, 'Napoleon made the mistake that was to cost him his throne' (p.80), since they lived to resist and in the end to overthrow him (see p.164).

- Above all, he mistakenly trusted Emperor Alexander I of Russia by granting peace at Tilsit (1807) when, according to Stendhal,

Napoleon could have destroyed Russia (p.153): 'If, the day after the peace of Tilsit, Napoleon's whole genius had been transformed into plain common sense, he would still be master of the better part of Europe' (p.161).

## Nemesis: disaster in Russia and defeat of the empire, 1812–14

According to the ancients, hubris led to nemesis, or retribution, whereby a man was brought down by his own faults. In Napoleon's case, Stendhal considered 'his ever mediocre political genius' (p.155) to be an immediate cause of the Russian debacle of 1812. This legendary catastrophe – the retreat from Moscow, marking the ruin of the *Grande Armée* and the turn of the tide for Napoleon – was the result of the irremediable 'arrogance and *crownomania*' (p.118) which blighted his judgement and blinded him to reality (see Figure 7.14). Napoleon provoked his own fate (p.158):

> Napoleon used to say: 'If I succeed in Russia, I shall be master of the whole world.' He let himself be defeated not by men, but by his own pride and by the climate, and Europe took up a new attitude. The minor princes ceased to tremble, the great sovereigns were no longer irresolute, and all looked to Russia, which had become the centre of an invincible opposition.

The retreat from Moscow was the beginning of the end. Sixteen months later Napoleon's French empire was no more. Such a rapid debacle suggests its inherent vulnerability. French rule, as Napoleon himself asserted, depended on maintaining his personal ascendancy by the prestige of continual victory. After the capitulation of a French force of 20,000 to the Spaniards at Bailen in 1808 (which reduced Napoleon to despair, according to Stendhal, p.111) and the incomparably greater Russian disaster of 1812, Napoleon's reputation for invincibility was fatally undermined.

Even so, the French empire was by no means doomed to destruction. Rather, France fell victim to Napoleon's temperament. In chapter 58 Stendhal points out Napoleon's political errors of judgement in 1813, but for which 'the whole Russian campaign would have been saved; that is to say, as far as France was concerned the empire would not have been broken up' (p.160). These errors were followed in turn by 'a mass of colossal mistakes' (p.160), a 'total eclipse of common sense' (p.162). Attributing this decline to Napoleon's hubris, Stendhal observes: 'Familiarity with the throne had increased the man's pride and lessened his common sense, which had been so remarkable in his early years' (p.162). As Stendhal notes, Napoleon had always been prone to 'fits of temper' and 'impatience' (p.119) if his judgement was questioned. See p.167 for Stendhal's perception of 'a final fit of temper and

*Figure 7.14 Anne-Louis Girodet-Trioson,* Napoleon I in St Cloud on 13 April 1812, *1812, Pierre noire, Musées de Châteauroux. Photo: reproduced by courtesy of Musées de Châteauroux.*

*'Prosperity had gradually altered and vitiated his character' (LN, pp.115–16).*

thoughtlessness which ultimately destroyed France and which posterity will find difficult to believe, so closely allied was it to folly.' In a word, Stendhal once more concludes, 'he was mad' (p.171).

Napoleon refused to compromise with the Coalition powers (Britain, Russia, Prussia and Austria), even when offered generous terms at the beginning of 1813 and still moderate terms – France's natural frontiers – at the end of 1813. He rejected any diminution of territory. He became a gambler, staking everything on the luck of the next battle. With him it was all or nothing, and in the end, of course, he lost all. France in 1814 was reduced to her boundaries of 1792, and in 1815 – after Waterloo – to those of 1789 by the Congress of Vienna (see Figure 7.15). Stendhal's criticism of Napoleon's unbending refusal to compromise was mixed with admiration, however, since such obstinacy in Stendhal's view also reflected a heroic character: 'That was indubitably the mistake of a great spirit, the misconception of a hero! And in it lay the whole secret of his conduct' (p.170). Napoleon went to his doom in a manner to appeal to the Romantics – defying insuperable odds, heavily outnumbered by the Allies, seeking a death in battle which constantly eluded him, and forever following his 'star' (see p.171).

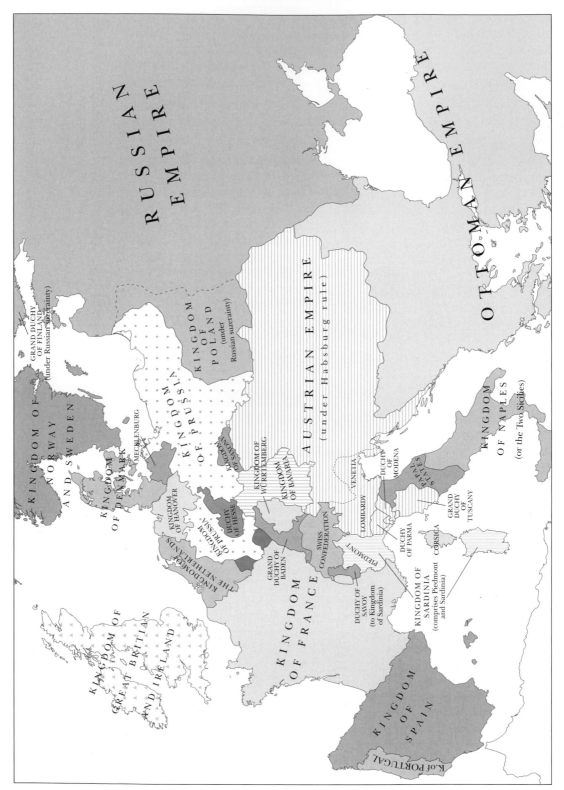

*Figure 7.15   (see caption facing page)*

*Figure 7.15   Europe in 1815 after the Congress of Vienna*

*After Napoleon's first abdication in May 1814, Russia, Britain, Austria and Prussia convened an international Congress at Vienna in September to settle the shape of post-Napoleonic Europe. Interrupted by the Hundred Days, its work continued and the final terms were agreed in June 1815.*

*The French empire was dismantled. France was restored to its 1792 frontiers under the first Treaty of Paris (May 1814) and to its 1789 frontiers under the second Treaty of Paris (November 1815). An allied army of occupation was stationed in France and France was to pay an indemnity.*

*Buffer-states were positioned next to France to guarantee the peace. Holland, the former Austrian Netherlands (Belgium) and Luxembourg were joined to form the kingdom of the Netherlands. An enlarged Prussia extended its territory to the Rhine. The kingdom of Sardinia (Piedmont and Sardinia) was restored. Austria retook Lombardy and was given Venetia and control of Tuscany, Parma and Modena. Old Regime monarchs were restored to France, Spain, Portugal, Holland, the kingdom of Naples and the kingdom of Sardinia. The Pope recovered the Papal States. Russia retained Finland and territory taken from Turkey and took over a core of Polish territory as the kingdom of Poland. Denmark ceded Norway to Sweden. Britain took fresh colonial possessions overseas. A loose German Confederation of 40 states, coterminous with the former Holy Roman Empire, was established under Austrian and Prussian influence. Overall, the 1815 settlement was monitored by the Great Powers (known as the Concert of Europe), and Russia and Austria subscribed to the Holy Alliance, a commitment to maintaining 'legitimacy' and to suppressing liberal movements in Europe.*

# 9   The impact of tyranny

Napoleon sometimes spoke approvingly of 'liberal government' and 'liberal ideas' (letter to Jérôme, 1807, in Anthology I, pp.109–10) and of 'liberal opinions', which, he declared from St Helena, 'will rule the universe' and which he claimed to have championed (Anthology I, p.117).

For Stendhal, though, however enlightened, Napoleon was no champion of 'liberal ideas' in the sense of ideas favourable to individual freedom, open political debate and popular representation. Rather, Napoleon's 'tyranny' gradually affected the morale and conduct of his imperial civil service, his ministers and the French people as a whole, including the army, on which his success ultimately depended. His centralization of the administration – whereby he ruled through departmental prefects appointed by him from Paris, while at the same time local issues that should have been decided on the spot were referred back to Paris for decision-making – led to bureaucratic absurdities and mountains of paperwork (chapter 46). By 1813, the French, in Stendhal's view, were 'a great people whose spirit was destroyed by a disheartening tyranny' (p.159); 'in fourteen years of administration, he had degraded men's hearts' (p.165).

Thus, on his return from Elba in 1815, Napoleon could no longer inspire 'people who for fourteen successive years had grown used to being ruled by a rod of iron and to cherish no other feeling than fear of losing their stipends' (p.211). He had driven away such independent-minded men as would have served him. Stendhal strikingly concludes: 'Napoleon had no men of ability because he wanted none' (p.216). He resorted to toadies, 'who destroyed him far more than did the battle of Waterloo' (p.215). 'Such men show how far he had already been corrupted by tyranny. At the time of Marengo [1800] he would have repudiated them with scorn' (p.215). Contemplating the increasing servility of Napoleon's ministers, Stendhal significantly concludes: 'When one sees the consequences of this, one comes almost to rejoice at the fall of Napoleon' (p.215).

## Control of the press

You may remember from Unit 6 the insistence of the revolutionaries of 1789 on freedom of the press. Article 11 of the Declaration of the Rights of Man and Citizen declared emphatically that 'the free expression of thoughts and opinions is one of the most precious of the rights of man; every citizen is therefore entitled to freedom of speech, of expression and of the press' (Anthology I, p.78).

Stendhal notes that the press under Napoleon 'was persecuted and subdued' (p.58) and that 'in the emperor's hands the press became a means of vilifying or degrading any man who had incurred his displeasure' (p.132). The letter from Napoleon to Fouché (Anthology I, p.107) gives a clear idea of Napoleon's attitude to the French press and his resolve to keep it under tight police supervision. He instructs Fouché to remind the editors of the few remaining Paris newspapers which he allowed to function – he reduced them from 73 to 13 in 1800, and in 1811 to four – that 'the revolutionary times are over'. Not merely would he not permit the divisive and demagogic excesses of the revolutionary papers, but also, he said, 'I shall never tolerate the newspapers to say or do anything against my interests.'

Napoleon took direct control of propaganda through the press and censorship in order 'to control public opinion, and ... to formulate favourable as well as to prevent unfavourable opinion' (Holtman, 1967, p.163). The *Moniteur* became his personal organ of propaganda, to which the ministers of police and the interior contributed articles on internal affairs, while Napoleon himself frequently dictated the military communiqués (*Bulletins de la Grande Armée*), selective in content and tendentious in comment. French losses in battle were played down; enemy casualties were exaggerated. No mention was made of Nelson's victory at Trafalgar in 1805, which assured British mastery at sea. Napoleon's final bulletin, issued after Waterloo, claimed that 'the battle had been won' when victory was lost by 'a sudden panic terror' (Barnett, 1997, p.210). 'The truth', Napoleon once remarked, 'is not half so important as what people think to be true' (Holtman, 1950, p.v): hence, as Napoleon himself admitted, the French expression 'lying like a bulletin' (Las Cases, 1999, vol.2, p.102).

## Oppression abroad and the rise of national feeling: Germany

What was Napoleon's attitude to press freedom in French-occupied Europe?

**EXERCISE**      Read the letter from Fouché to the police superintendent at Hamburg, 1811 (Anthology I, p.112). What does it suggest about Napoleon's attitude to the press in the non-French departments of the empire? (Hamburg, in the specially created department of the Bouches-de-l'Elbe, had just been annexed.)

**DISCUSSION**   Napoleon was clearly determined to suppress not merely any overt expression of political opposition but even works of literature likely 'to disturb the social order by undermining the respect due to lawful authority' in the newly annexed departments. He sought, in other words, to stamp out any expression of anti-French sentiment.

**EXERCISE**      Why do you suppose the works proscribed in Fouché's letter are plays?

**DISCUSSION**   In contrast to novels or poems, plays might be considered particularly dangerous because they were likely to be read or acted by assembled groups. If publicly performed, their tendency might be to incite the audience.

Napoleon paid close attention to control of the stage. (He was particularly sensitive to personal criticism and ridicule: see LN, pp.139–40.) Before permitting the first performance in France of Mozart's *Don Giovanni* in 1805, he consulted Fouché about its likely effect on public opinion (Holtman, 1950, pp.160–1). See the letter from Napoleon to Berthier, 1807 (Anthology I, pp.108–9), and note his extraordinarily high-handed demand to the King of Prussia to execute the ringleaders of a peaceful anti-French protest.

All three of the plays by Schiller which Fouché ordered to be suppressed were key works of pre-Romanticism and Romanticism with obvious contemporary implications. *The Robbers* (1781), the most popular drama of the *Sturm und Drang* movement, concerned rebellion and murder by idealistic young men (see Unit 1, pp.44–5); *Maria Stuart* (1800) concerned the tragic captive-heroine and *William Tell* (1804) the Swiss struggle for national liberation from foreign tyranny. As a devotee of the French classical theatre, Napoleon was aware of the appeal of drama as a moral agent, a call to action. The works of Schiller, who had been honoured by the National Assembly in 1792 in token of his revolutionary credentials, exerted a particular appeal to national feeling in French-occupied Germany and Austria. Stendhal tells us that Friedrich Staps, the student from Saxony who attempted to assassinate Napoleon in 1809, had 'a volume of Schiller in his pocket' (LN, p.85).[28]

On p.85 Stendhal mentions the judicial murder in 1806 of Johannes Palm, the Nuremberg bookseller executed for selling *Germany in her Deep Humiliation,* a pamphlet protesting against Napoleon's oppression of Germany. Napoleon had him court-martialled and shot. Stendhal singles this out as an act so heinous as almost to justify Napoleon's sufferings in St Helena, commenting 'let despotism do what it will, it cannot destroy the printed word' (p.85).

Anthology I, pp.109–10, contains Napoleon's advice in 1807 to his brother Jérôme, king of the newly created state of Westphalia (intended as a model for imitation by the other client-states of the Confederation of the Rhine, of which Napoleon was 'Protector'). The letter provides clear evidence of Napoleon's assumption of the superiority of French laws, institutions and administrative methods and their exportability. 'What people would wish to return to the arbitrary government of Prussia when they have tasted the benefits of wise and liberal administration?' he confidently asks. Note his claim to know the desires of 'the peoples of Germany, as well as those of France, Italy and Spain'.

It is true that northern Italy, western Germany and the Low Countries (but not Spain) had a substantial middle class which welcomed Napoleon's reforms and actively collaborated with the French. His would-be assassin, Friedrich Staps, told him that originally 'I was one of your greatest admirers' (Anthology I, p.112). However, Napoleon's insistence on the application of French models, his assumption of the superiority of France as *la Grande Nation*, his policy of 'France first' (*la France avant tout)* (Herold, 1955, p.186) and his increasingly oppressive rule were resented almost everywhere, even by those who originally welcomed the French.

Napoleon's rule was characterized by military and economic exploitation: recruitment for the *Grande Armée*, billeting of troops on the locals, living

[28] Why Goethe's *Faust* was included in the category of proscribed works may become clearer when you study it later in the course.

off the country, heavy taxation, and the constraints on trade imposed by the Continental System. From 1804 to 1814 it is reckoned that roughly one-half of France's military expenditure derived from tribute levied from conquered states (Sutherland, 1985, p.413). The *Grande Armée* was supplemented by large non-French contingents, 718,000 in all between 1805 and 1814, of which Italy furnished 121,000, Bavaria 110,000 and Poland 85,000. Italian casualties were highest pro rata, the Italians losing 60 per cent of their men. The German client-states in the Confederation of the Rhine – Bavaria, Saxony, Westphalia, Württemberg, Berg and Baden, in particular (Austria and Prussia only provided troops for the Russian campaign) – furnished 366,500 men and lost approximately 62,000 or 17 per cent (Castelot, 1989, vol.3, p.1506). The *Grande Armée* which invaded Russia in 1812 – the largest army in history hitherto – comprised between 500,000 and 650,000 men, of whom roughly one-half consisted of non-French contingents. Of these, some 18,000 stragglers, French and non-French, returned (Tulard, 1977, pp.394, 407; Martin, 2001, p.258; Godechot, Hislop and Dowd, 1971, p.181).

From the documents on the assassination attempt (Anthology I, pp.110–12) we can see Napoleon's bewilderment, apparently quite genuine, that any German should seek to murder him. This would seem to confirm his cosmopolitan (albeit French-centred) outlook derived from the Enlightenment. His only explanation was that his would-be assassin, Staps, was insane or a fanatic. In Germany, however, Staps and Johannes Palm became martyrs in the increasingly popular cause of national feeling. See Figure 7.16 and Napoleon's unsigned decree of 1813 (Anthology I, p.114) for evidence of his unpopularity in Germany and his readiness to resort to ruthless reprisals against uprisings in the Rhineland departments of the empire during the German 'War of Liberation' of 1813. Napoleon used harsh methods throughout Europe to deter and punish resistance, particularly in Spain, as you will recall from Video 2, band 1, and in Goya's *Third of May 1808* (see Illustrations Book, Plate V2.6).

*'Befreiungskrieg'*

National consciousness in Germany developed in reaction to the experience of French occupation. It was fostered by thinkers like August Wilhelm Schlegel (1767–1845) and Johann Gottlieb Fichte (1762–1814), who turned against Napoleon, albeit reluctantly, to preach resistance. Fichte did so in 1808 in a series of *Addresses to the German Nation*. Ernst Moritz Arndt (1769–1860) stirred national sentiment with his songs and poems, such as 'Vaterlandslied' ('Song of the Fatherland') and 'Was ist das deutsche Vaterland?' ('What is the German Fatherland?') and helped to found the patriotic student association, the *Tugendbund* (League of Virtue), an organization half-deplored, half-admired by Stendhal for its 'burning zeal' and 'patriotic enthusiasm' (pp.81, 171). Between one-fifth and one-half of the student body in north German universities alone enlisted against the French (Rowe, 2001, p.221). Goethe, it was true, remained an admirer of Napoleon and proudly sported the Legion of Honour bestowed on him. For Goethe, Napoleon represented a higher

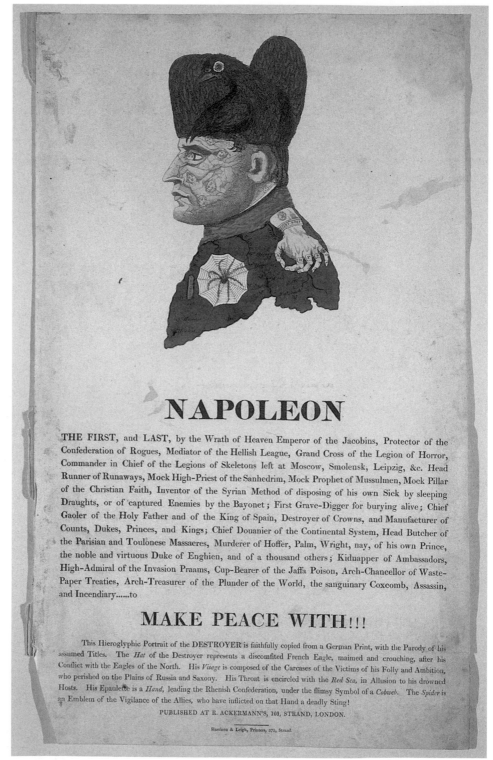

*Figure 7.16 (see caption facing page)*

*Figure 7.16  R. Ackermann,* Napoleon: The First and Last ..., *1814, engraving and letter print, Heber Mardon Collection, Devon Local Studies Library, Exeter. Photo: courtesy of Devon Library and Information Services.*

*This cartoon is from a German original, 1813, entitled* Triumph des Jahres: Den Deutschen zum Neuenjahr *(A Year of Triumph: A New Year's Gift for the Germans). The mock-titles parody Napoleon's actual titles (such as Protector of the Confederation of the Rhine, Mediator of the Swiss Confederation). Other mock-titles allude to the 'crimes' discussed by Stendhal.*

*'This man whom ... the English and Madame de Staël present as Machiavellianism personified, as one of the incarnations of evil ...' (LN, p.164).*

level of European civilization and the German resistance was essentially reactionary.[29]

Napoleon's armies were, in fact, brought down by Old Regime armies: Russian, Austrian and German peasant conscripts led by princes and nobles and Wellington's army of what he called 'the scum of the earth'. But the peoples too were actively provoked to resist. Napoleon 'was facing the collective will of peoples whose sense of nationality he had helped to arouse, as well as the determination of the dynasts to restore their supremacy' (Davies, 1997, p.744). Moreover, while nationalism was an aspect of Romanticism cultivated mainly by intellectuals and middle-class youth, the peoples at large were animated by instinctive hostility against the French as invaders and against the enlightened reforms which they imposed. In Frankfurt, where there were street riots in 1807, and in the Austrian Tyrol, which rose up in 1809 under the peasant leader Andreas Hofer, attacks were mounted on Jews, perceived as beneficiaries of Napoleon's reforms.

Overall hostility to the French was particularly lasting and virulent in Spain (Stendhal brings this out vividly in chapters 36–9 and 41–2), where national resistance largely partook of hatred for the modernity which Napoleon sought to impose on a backward-looking nation, fiercely attached to its religion and traditions. Napoleon believed that 'the Spaniards are like other peoples and are not a class apart' (quoted in Markham, 1975, p.153, and see LN, p.114). In Stendhal's words: 'The writers of slanders accuse Napoleon of having had too great a contempt for mankind. Here we see him committing a grave error because he had too high an opinion of the Spaniards' (p.98).

---

[29] Beethoven too, despite his earlier antipathy, came to respect Napoleon's achievement. 'As a German I have been his greatest enemy, but actual conditions have reconciled me to him. He understood art and science and despised ignorance' (*c.*1820, quoted in Barzun, 2000, p.484).

## Napoleon and the liberal opposition

> Bred on military ideas, to him discussion always seemed like insubordination. Experience proved to him daily his immense personal superiority, and he despised men too much to let them discuss measures which he had deemed salutary.

(LN, p.53)

We noted earlier what Stendhal called Napoleon's 'shaky republicanism'. This included a rooted aversion to – and indeed the suppression of – political opposition, for which he left no institutional outlet. As Stendhal says, 'Napoleon was not used to opposition' (p.92). Nor did he tolerate criticism. Napoleon disliked intellectuals: 'metaphysicians' or 'ideologues' as he contemptuously termed them. These 'ideologues' included several senators, notably the philosopher Antoine-Louis Claude Destutt de Tracy (1754–1836), much admired by Stendhal, who refers to him several times in *A Life of Napoleon* and regarded his *Commentary on Montesquieu's 'On the Spirit of the Laws'* (1817) as 'the last word in political science and hence my political credo' (Stendhal, 1986, p.358). Other 'ideologue' senators included Sieyès, who drafted the 1799 constitution ('the wise and good Sieyès', Stendhal writes, p.48), the historian Volney, and Lanjuinais. These men, says Stendhal, 'had attracted too much attention by their dangerous and liberal opinions' (p.129). The modern historian Jean Tulard calls them 'the last adherents of the philosophy of the Enlightenment' (1977, p.280). It is also the case that the greatest writers of the time, Chateaubriand (1768–1848), Benjamin Constant (1767–1830) and Mme de Staël, though often torn between admiration and misgivings, ultimately came out against Napoleon, forming a kind of resistance of the intellectuals.

*[handwritten margin note: Stendhal follows Montesquieu]*

*[handwritten margin note: 16 when Napoleon declared himself First Consul.]*

## Mme de Staël

The most celebrated representative of the liberal opposition to Napoleon was Germaine de Staël (1766–1817), Swiss born, Protestant, daughter of Jacques Necker, wealthy finance minister to Louis XVI (see Figure 7.17). Her marriage to the Swedish ambassador to France was a marriage of convenience, and her lovers included Talleyrand and the novelist Benjamin Constant, a fellow Swiss. Brought up on the *Encyclopédie,* Staël welcomed the Revolution until forced to emigrate in 1792. Returning in 1795, she hosted a glittering *salon* under the Directory which became 'a seminary of political opposition and liberal opinions' (Ellis, 1997, p.182).

Staël recognized Napoleon's genius and tried to win him over during the consulate. Napoleon professed a low opinion of women generally (perhaps, as Stendhal suggests, from feelings of inferiority: see p.141), and of intellectual women and Mme de Staël in particular. Staël brought out the worst in him, provoking 'dramatic outbursts of Corsican

*Figure 7.17    Anonymous*, Germaine de Staël next to the Bust of her Father, *oil on canvas, Château de Coppet. Photo: reproduced by courtesy of Château de Coppet, Switzerland.*

'*Serve notice to that woman [Mme de Staël] ... not to block my path ... Or else I shall break her, I shall crush her. Let her keep quiet, it's the wisest course she can take*' *(Napoleon, 1801, in Herold, 1959, p.225).*

'*Lift your head high in adversity and permit no man on earth, be he ever so powerful, to hold you under his boot*' *(Necker to his daughter, Germaine de Staël, on Napoleon's banishing her from France, 1803, in Herold, 1959, p.250).*

'*I shall defy his fury*' *(Mme de Staël, 1802, in Herold, 1959, p.227).*

'*I swore never to set foot in any country which was in any way subject to Emperor Napoleon*' *(Mme de Staël on taking asylum in Russia, July 1812, in Herold, 1959, p.413).*

machismo' (Lyons, 1994, p.140). Stendhal reports one such outburst (p.141). Furthermore, as Stendhal records, 'people who incurred his displeasure were threatened, arrested and banished without trial' (p.58). Staël was foremost among these.

Staël's lover, Benjamin Constant, was a spokesman for the minority opposition in the Tribunat. In 1802 Napoleon, for whom Constant was another 'ideologue', purged the Tribunat and removed Constant, who joined the unofficial opposition. At the same time Napoleon banned Staël from within 40 miles of Paris and placed her under police surveillance; in 1803 he exiled her from France altogether. The reason was her novel *Delphine* (1802), a plea for equality between the sexes and defiantly dedicated 'to France, silent but enlightened'.

Staël went into exile on her father's estate at Coppet in Switzerland, which became both a base for her European travels and a focus of liberal opposition to Napoleon, centring on herself, Constant, Mme Récamier and others, including Chateaubriand. She travelled to Italy and to Germany, meeting Goethe, Schiller and Schlegel. She continued to defy and to infuriate Napoleon, publishing *Corinne* (1807), feminist, pro-British and a plea for constitutional government.

Staël's main work is *De l'Allemagne (On Germany),* one of the seminal works of European Romanticism, challenging French assumptions of cultural supremacy and implicitly sympathetic to Germany's plight under French occupation. As with *Corinne,* while Napoleon's name is never mentioned in *De l'Allemagne,* 'hatred of the Emperor is at the heart of this book' (Heinrich Heine, quoted in Furst, 1979, pp.63–4). It was about to appear in Paris in 1810 when Napoleon had all 10,000 copies seized and pulped (it was finally published in London in 1813). Napoleon had Staël placed under house arrest at Coppet. His minister of police, Savary, wrote to her:

> Your exile is the natural consequence of the course you have followed for several years. It seemed to me that the air of this country [France] did not agree with you – and we have not yet reached the point where we have to model ourselves on the nations you admire. Your last work is un-French.

> (3 October 1810, quoted in Herold, 1959, p.390)

In 1812, giving Napoleon's police the slip, Staël travelled to Austria, Russia, Sweden and England, where she spent over a year, meeting, among others, Byron and Wilberforce (and lending her support to the anti-slavery campaign). In each country she rallied support and even liaised between the leaders of the allied coalition against Napoleon, whom she hoped to see replaced by his former colleague Marshal Bernadotte, now heir to the throne of Sweden.[30] After Napoleon's first

---

[30] The joke went the rounds that there were three Great Powers in post-Napoleonic Europe: Britain, Russia and Mme de Staël (Furst, 1979, p.56).

abdication in 1814 she returned to Paris, where she remained during the Hundred Days (she deplored the Bourbon reaction no less than Napoleon's rule). She died at Coppet in 1817 and her *Reflections on the Main Events of the French Revolution* appeared posthumously in 1818.

In the extracts from her *Reflections on ... the French Revolution* (Anthology I, pp.118–21) Staël shows her attachment to the ideals of 1789 and to humane, liberal and personal values. She equated the Revolution with the cause of personal freedom and constitutional government, denounced the course of events after 1792, and tested Napoleon's record against her criteria and convictions.

**EXERCISE**

Consider Staël's verdicts on Napoleon. Taking extracts (a) to (e) in the Anthology, identify in each case Staël's main charge against Napoleon.

**DISCUSSION**

(a) Napoleon's assumption of total control of the press.

(b) While 'the entire nation wanted a free and constitutional government', Napoleon reverted to an Old Regime style monarchy by assuming 'absolute power', harnessing the Church's blessing on himself and creating an imperial nobility. Staël sees this as a 'counter-revolution'.

(c) Napoleon's responsibility for the death of the Duke d'Enghien.

(d) Napoleon's exploitation of the non-French departments and client-states of the empire.

(e) Napoleon's avowal that his priorities in Europe were himself and France.

## Stendhal and Staël

**EXERCISE**

How persuasive do you find Staël's critiques of Napoleon? Your answers will depend partly on the evidence at your disposal, partly on your own outlook and attitude to Napoleon. (I have summarized Stendhal's attitude where appropriate in the discussion below.)

**DISCUSSION**

(a) Staël is factually correct. As we have seen, freedom of the press was rigorously controlled, monopolized and systematically exploited by Napoleon. Stendhal is ambivalent about press freedom. On p.85 he unequivocally condemns Napoleon's execution of the German bookseller Palm, but on pp.59 and 77 he appears somewhat cynically to justify Napoleon's restrictions on press freedom.

(b)  We cannot be certain what 'the entire nation' wanted in 1799 other than (presumably) stability after ten years of revolutionary turmoil. The plebiscites of 1802 and 1804 suggest public support for Napoleon's accretion of power (though recent research also suggests that the plebiscites were rigged). Stendhal argues that the choice in 1799 was between Napoleon and the Bourbons and that his 'arbitrary measures' as First Consul were justified in self-defence (p.53). Staël's claim that the Catholic clergy in France 'preached despotism' seems fair comment given their acceptance of Napoleon's *Imperial Catechism*, but it also reflects her Protestant bias.

(c)  By eliminating the Duke d'Enghien Napoleon sought to make clear that there would be no Bourbon restoration and to deter royalist conspiracies. Staël states that the murder was a 'crime' and marked a fatal turning-point in Napoleon's career. Stendhal in part (and Napoleon himself) justified the murder as a political necessity (chapters 25, 27–9, 31).

(d)  Staël accepts that Napoleon's rule brought benefits to Europe, but argues that it was based on exploitation and alienated all the non-French states. Stendhal insists on the benefits of French administration.

(e)  Napoleon appears indeed to reveal himself as an egotist. Stendhal goes further in claiming that 'unhindered arrogance' affected his judgement.

---

As one who served the Napoleonic regime, Stendhal was not associated with the liberal opposition. However, he seems to have shared some of their republican convictions – so at least he said in retrospect. He shows approval of George Washington (pp.52–3). He says that it would have been better for free institutions had Napoleon been assassinated on or within a few years of 18th Brumaire (pp.49, 51). He agrees that the consulate was 'a military despotism' (p.51). He sympathizes with Napoleon's political rival, General Moreau; indeed he later claimed that he himself had taken part in the conspiracy for which Moreau was exiled in 1804 (LN, pp.63–4, 69–70, 73, 77; Strickland, 1974, p.102). He enjoins the reader to 'remember the admirable conspiracy of General Malet' (p.137 footnote), who in 1812 made a daring attempt to restore the republic during Napoleon's absence in Russia.

Notwithstanding Napoleon's professed allegiance to 'liberal opinions' (Anthology I, p.117), Stendhal points out 'his rage against all that was truly liberal' (LN, p.215). In particular, Stendhal regrets Napoleon's total aversion to 'representative government', which he calls 'this sublime invention' (p.214). Contending that Napoleon's education was defective, Stendhal speculates what might have happened if, instead of being 'bred on military ideas' (p.53), Napoleon had read Hume and Montesquieu:

- 'He might, perhaps, have grasped the strength which public opinion confers upon a government' (p.23).

- 'If he had understood the invincible power which government by public opinion confers ...' (p.53).

- 'He might have established the republic' (p.54).

As it was, Napoleon had no real sympathy with liberal institutions. After 18th Brumaire, Stendhal argues, 'he did not consider how much authority could safely be entrusted to the people; he sought to discover with how little power they would be content' (p.54). For all the merits of his administration – and Stendhal also illustrates its bureaucratic excesses in chapter 46 – he concludes with bitter irony (p.120):

> But the main idea was to humble the citizen and above all to prevent him from *political discussion*, an abominable habit contracted by the French in the days of Jacobinism. Without such jealous precautions, that other monster ... abhorred by all the successive French governments which have exploited France, might have reappeared – and by this I mean *public opinion*.

A comparison between Staël and Stendhal suggests that despite significant differences of approach, in many respects there was much common ground in their criticism of Napoleon. Stendhal's repeated denunciation of Staël's book as a 'slander' therefore seems somewhat surprising. A possible explanation for his hostility to Staël is that, as the obscure author of a yet unfinished biography of Napoleon, Stendhal, who felt proprietorial towards the subject of his book, was irritated at the thought that Staël had beaten him to publication. He, a little-known tyro, had been upstaged by 'the leading talent of the age' (p.21), one of France's most distinguished and influential writers, a respected liberal known for her principled resistance to Napoleon.

A second and related possibility, suggested earlier, is that in his desire to be original at all costs, Stendhal deliberately adopted views opposed to those of Staël. Take, for example, his defence of Napoleon's police (chapter 66). Knowing that Staël had been put under police surveillance and exiled by Napoleon, Stendhal not only contrasted the leniency of Napoleon's police with the 'White Terror' unleashed under the restoration, but also attacked Staël – somewhat unfairly – as an apologist for the Bourbon reaction. His *Life of Napoleon* suggests that he shared her basic reservations about Napoleon, but that he reacted vigorously to her exposé of his hero by leaping to Napoleon's defence as 'the writer' who 'feels the need to respect what he admires and what for so long he did respect' (p.174 footnote).

'Slander' - More to it than this.
Staël writes from a position of royalty and aristocracy. This is the 'slander'. Stendhal is from lower rank, similar to Napoleon, and therefore can write truthfully of his motives. Staël can't. That is the 'slander'. Stendhal wants to correct the misrepresentations of N. borne of Staël's class.

# 10   Conclusion

Stendhal applauded the Revolution for abolishing the privileges of nobility and church. He deplored what he calls 'the mixture of Catholicism and aristocracy' (p.38) which had characterized French society from the seventeenth century to the Revolution, and he denounced the attempts by the *ultras* under the restoration to put the clock back to before 1789. (The restoration Bourbons in fact retained the centralized administration left by Napoleon and proved unable to reverse the social changes brought by the Revolution.)

In many ways Napoleon may plausibly be considered a nineteenth-century analogue to eighteenth-century 'enlightened absolutism'. In making this comparison, however, we should not lose sight of the gulf that separated him from pre-revolutionary France. Frederick the Great, Catherine the Great and Joseph II ruled over the hierarchical society of the Old Regime. At its apex was the nobility, whose privileges they upheld. 'I am an aristocrat,' declared Catherine, 'it is my profession' (Lentin, 1985, p.xx). Napoleon invited back the old nobility and in 1808 created an imperial nobility of his own, but he never contemplated restoring the pre-1789 privileges. On the contrary, in his coronation oath of 1804 he swore to protect, and he did protect, the rights of the beneficiaries of the Revolution, men (including nobles) who had become property owners by buying up estates formerly belonging to the Church and nobility. These landowners, who paid the highest levels of taxation, were categorized as 'notables'. It was, above all, on the support of these 100,000 landowning 'notables' – 'the masses of granite', he called them (Broers, 1996, p.57) – that Napoleon founded the social basis of his regime.

*a middle class*

At St Helena Napoleon claimed he had always believed that 'sovereignty lay in the people' and that 'the imperial government was a kind of republic' (Anthology I, p.115). His defeat at Waterloo, he said, represented the triumph of 'the cause of kings against peoples, of privilege against equality, of oligarchs against liberals, of the principles of the Holy Alliance against the sovereignty of the people' (Napoleon quoted by Gourgaud in de Clair, 1948, p.551). He also professed that it had been his intention to champion the cause of national unification in Germany and Italy (Anthology I, p.116). These bold claims were to prove an exceptionally potent ingredient of 'the Napoleonic phenomenon', especially in the period after 1815, but they remain highly controversial and call for measured consideration. By way of conclusion, therefore, let us focus once more on the basic charges levelled against Napoleon by the liberal opposition.

**EXERCISE**   Having now studied Napoleon's career, how far do you endorse his claim to be 'a son of the Revolution' (LN, p.140)? See the Declaration of the Rights of Man and Citizen, 1789 (Anthology I, pp.77–9) for a standard of comparison.

**DISCUSSION**   Despite his claims from St Helena, it is difficult to see Napoleon as motivated by respect for the personal freedoms proclaimed in 1789: freedom of speech, of the press, of association. Nor did he show himself a friend of representative government or political or ideological opposition, which he suppressed. Napoleon is best judged by what he did at the time rather than what he said about it later.

Napoleon believed in efficient government, not representative government. His original intentions towards the peoples of France and Europe seem to have been enlightened, and the reforms which he imposed proved lasting in the case of France and influenced much of Europe: the abolition of feudal privilege, equality before the law, religious toleration, trial by jury, equality of opportunity, legal codification and a modern centralized administration. This seems to be what Napoleon meant by 'liberal', that is, synonymous with 'enlightened'. But it was enlightenment from above, implemented in the spirit of eighteenth-century 'enlightened absolutism'; and his attitude to Europe, qualified as it was by his avowed policy of himself and France first, can be described at best as 'enlightened self-interest'.

The Declaration of the Rights of Man asserted that 'any society which lacks a sure guarantee of rights or a fixed separation of powers, has no constitution' (Anthology I, p.78). Under Napoleon there was no sure guarantee of rights and no separation of powers (executive, legislative and judicial) such as the Enlightenment philosopher Montesquieu had prescribed as a recipe against 'despotism', and which Sieyès had provided for in the constitution of 1799. By his highly personalized rule, Napoleon 'overturned perhaps the most fundamental republican principle of all: that power and authority, whether in the civil state or in the army, must not be concentrated in one man. The Napoleonic Empire was more like absolute monarchy under another name' (Ellis, 1997, p.53). Stendhal made the same point (p.54).

The French empire was a 'police state' in the sense that Napoleon monitored, controlled and directed public opinion through propaganda, censorship, police measures and a network of spies. The right of assembly was dependent on police permission (see LN, p.139). Napoleon re-established state prisons across the French empire in 1810 for the detention of suspects without trial – the re-establishment, as it were, of the Bastille and the *lettre de cachet*. But Stendhal's defence of Napoleon's treatment of political prisoners holds good: 'the state prisons were less full than under good King Louis XVI' (p.58). The eight designated 'state prisons' housed 640 detainees in 1814, of whom half were political prisoners (Sutherland, 1985, p.391).

By comparison both with the reign of Terror and with what would follow – the dictatorships of the nineteenth, twentieth and twenty-first centuries – Napoleon's regime was, as Stendhal insists, generally mild in the exercise of its repressive and punitive powers. Napoleon's treatment of Mme de Staël, though bullying, compares very favourably with the suppression of liberals in restoration Europe, to say nothing of later political dissidents. As Napoleon said on Elba, 'had I felt less repugnance for bloodshed, perhaps I would not be here now' (LN, p.68). Let Stendhal have the last word: 'There was a tyrant, but little despotism. Nevertheless, civilization's real cry is "No despotism!"' (p.58).

# References

Agulhon, M. (1981) *Marianne into Battle: Republican Imagery and Symbolism in France, 1789–1880*, trans. J. Lloyd, Cambridge, Cambridge University Press.

Alexander, R.S. (1995) 'Napoleon Bonaparte and the French Revolution', in P. Pilbeam (ed.) *Themes in Modern European History 1780–1830*, London and New York, Routledge, pp.40–64.

Alexander, R.S. (2001) *Napoleon*, London, Edward Arnold.

Anderson, M. (1985) *The Ascendancy of Europe 1815–1914*, Harlow, Longman.

Aubry, O. (1935) *Sainte-Hélène*, 2 vols, Paris, Flammarion.

Bainbridge, S. (1995) *Napoleon and English Romanticism*, Cambridge, Cambridge University Press.

Bainville, J. (1938) *Napoleon*, London, Jonathan Cape.

Barnett, C. (1997) *Bonaparte*, Ware, Wordsworth (first published 1978).

Barzun, J. (2000) *From Dawn to Decadence: 500 Years of Western Cultural Life*, New York, Harper Collins.

Bessand-Massenet, P. (1978) *Quand la France attendait Bonaparte 1794–1800*, Paris, Librairie Académique.

Bluche, F. (1981) *Le Bonapartisme*, in 'Que sais-je?' series, Paris, Presses universitaires de France.

Broers, M. (1996) *Europe under Napoleon 1799–1815*, London, Edward Arnold.

Brookner, A. (2000) *Romanticism and its Discontents*, London, Viking.

Bruun, G. (1967) *The Enlightened Despots*, 2nd edn, New York, Holt, Rinehart and Winston.

Castelot, A. (1989) *Grande Histoire Illustrée de Napoléon*, 3 vols, Paris, Bordas.

Chandler, D. (1999) *Dictionary of the Napoleonic Wars*, Ware, Wordsworth (first published 1979).

Clair, S. de (ed.) (1948) *Napoleon's Memoirs*, London, Faber.

Connelly, O. (1969) *Napoleon's Satellite Kingdoms*, New York, Free Press.

Connelly, O. (1999) *Blundering to Glory: Napoleon's Military Campaigns,* Wilmington, Scholarly Resources.

Davies, N. (1997) *Europe: A History,* London, Pimlico.

Del Litto, V. (1962) *La Vie intellectuelle de Stendhal: Genèse et évolution de ses idées (1802–1821)*, Paris, Presses universitaires de France.

Dwyer, P. (2001a) 'Napoleon and the drive for glory: reflections on the making of French foreign policy', in P. Dwyer (ed.) *Napoleon and Europe*, Harlow, Longman, pp.118–35.

Dwyer, P. (ed.) (2001b) *Napoleon and Europe,* Harlow, Longman.

Ellis G. (1997) *Napoleon,* Harlow, Longman.

Fisher, H.A.L. (1971) *Napoleon,* Oxford, Oxford University Press (first published 1912).

Furst, L.R. (1979) *The Contours of European Romanticism*, London, Macmillan.

Gendzier, S.J. (ed. and trans.) (1967) *Denis Diderot's 'The Encyclopedia': Selections*, New York, Harper and Row.

Geyl, P. (1965) *Napoleon: For and Against,* Harmondsworth, Penguin (first published 1949).

Godechot, J. (1968) *Les Institutions de la France sous la Révolution et l'Empire*, Paris, Presses universitaires de France.

Godechot, J., Hyslop, B. and Dowd, D. (1971) *The Napoleonic Era in Europe,* New York, Holt, Rinehart and Winston.

Gooch, G.P. (1931) *Studies in Modern History,* London, Longmans, Green & Co.

Gourgaud, G. (1932) *The St Helena Story,* trans. H. Belloc, London, Bodley Head.

Green, F.C. (1939) *Stendhal,* Cambridge, Cambridge University Press.

Guérard, A. (1956) *France in the Classical Age: The Life and Death of an Ideal*, New York, Harper Torchbooks (first published 1928).

Hampson, N. (1969) *The First European Revolution 1776–1815*, London, Thames and Hudson.

Heisler, M. (1969) *Stendhal et Napoléon,* Paris, éditions A-G Nizet.

Hemmings, F.W. (1966) *Stendhal: A Study of his Novels,* Oxford, Clarendon Press.

Hemmings, F.W.J. (1987) *Culture and Society in France 1789–1848*, Leicester, Leicester University Press.

Herold, J.C. (ed.) (1955) *The Mind of Napoleon: A Selection from his Written and Spoken Words*, New York, Columbia University Press.

Herold J.C. (1959) *Mistress to an Age: A Life of Madame de Staël*, London, Hamish Hamilton.

Holtman, R.B. (1950) *Napoleonic Propaganda*, New York, Greenwood Press.

Holtman, R.B. (1967) *The Napoleonic Revolution*, Philadelphia, J.B. Lippincott.

Hugo, V. (1985) *Oeuvres Complètes, poésie I*, Paris, éditions Robert Laffont.

Jourdan, A. (1998) *Napoléon: Héros, imperator, mécène*, Paris, Aubier.

Lange, V. (1982) *The Classical Age of German Literature 1740–1815*, London, Edward Arnold.

Las Cases, E. de (1999) *Mémorial de Sainte Hélène*, 4 vols, Paris, éditions le grand livre du mois (first published 1823).

Lean, E.T. (1970) *The Napoleonists: A Study in Political Disaffection 1760–1900*, Oxford, Oxford University Press.

Lentin, A. (1985) *Enlightened Absolutism (1760–1790): A Documentary Sourcebook*, Newcastle-upon-Tyne, Avero Publications.

Lentz, T. (1999) *Le Grand Consulat 1799–1804,* Paris, Librairie Arthème Fayard.

Lyons, M. (1994) *Napoleon Bonaparte and the Legacy of the French Revolution*, London, Macmillan.

Markham, F. (1963) *Napoleon*, London, Weidenfeld and Nicolson.

Markham, F. (1975) *The Bonapartes*, London, Weidenfeld and Nicolson.

Martin, A. (2001) 'The Russian empire and the Napoleonic Wars', in P. Dwyer (ed.) *Napoleon and Europe,* Harlow, Longman, pp.243–63.

Martineau, G. (1976) *Napoleon's Last Journey,* trans. F. Partridge, London, John Murray.

Martineau, H. (1950) *Le Calendrier de Stendhal,* Paris, Le Divan.

Martineau, H. (1952) *Le Coeur de Stendhal,* vol.1, 1783–1821, Paris, éditions Albin Michel.

Maury, R. and Candé-Montholon, F. de (2000) *L'énigme Napoléon résolue: L'extraordinaire découverte des documents Montholon,* Paris, éditions Albin Michel.

Michel, A. and Lavoix, H. (1897) 'L'Art en Europe jusqu'en 1814', in E. Lavisse and A. Rambaud (eds) *Napoleon 1800–1815,* Paris, Armand Colin & Cie.

Parker, H.T. (1937) *The Cult of Antiquity and the French Revolutionaries,* Chicago, University of Chicago Press.

Richardson, F. (1974) *Napoleon's Death: An Inquest,* London, William Kimber.

Robbins Landon, H.C. (ed.) (1970) *Beethoven: A Documentary Study,* London, Thames and Hudson.

Rowe, M. (2001) 'Napoleon and state formation in central Europe', in P. Dwyer (ed.) *Napoleon and Europe,* Harlow, Longman, pp.204–24.

Roy, C. (1968), *Stendhal par lui-même,* Paris, éditions du seuil.

Sibalis, M. (2001) 'The Napoleonic police state', in P. Dwyer (ed.) *Napoleon and Europe,* Harlow, Longman, pp.79–94.

Sorel, A. (1885–1904) *L'Europe et la Révolution Française,* 8 vols, Paris, Librairie Plon.

Stendhal (1962) 'Lord Byron in Italy: an eyewitness account', in *Racine and Shakespeare,* trans. G. Daniels, New York, Crowell-Collier Press (first published 1830).

Stendhal (1975) *Memoirs of an Egotist,* trans. D. Ellis, London, Chatto and Windus (first published 1832).

Stendhal (1986) *Vie de Napoléon,* ed. L. Royer, new edn by V. del Litto and E. Abravanel, in *Collection des Oeuvres Complètes de Stendhal,* vol.39, Geneva and Paris, Slatkin Reprints.

Stendhal (2004) *A Life of Napoleon* (LN), trans. R. Gant, ed. A. Lentin, Milton Keynes, The Open University.

Strickland, G. (1974) *Stendhal: The Education of a Novelist,* Cambridge, Cambridge University Press.

Sutherland, D.M. (1985) *France 1789–1815: Revolution and Counterrevolution,* London, Fontana.

Thornton, M.J. (1968) *Napoleon after Waterloo,* Stanford, Stanford University Press.

Tulard, J. (1977) *Napoléon ou le mythe du sauveur,* Paris, Fayard.

Weider, B. and Forshufvud, S. (1995) *Assassination at St Helena Revisited,* New York, John Wiley.

Weider, B. and Hapgood, D. (1982) *The Murder of Napoleon,* New York, Robson Books.

Whately, R. (1985) *Historic Doubts Relative to Napoleon Buonaparte,* Berkeley and London, Scolar Press (first published 1819).

Wolloch, I. (2001) 'The Napoleonic regime and French society', in P. Dwyer (ed.) *Napoleon and Europe*, Harlow, Longman, pp.60–78.

# Further reading

## Primary sources

Herold, J.C. (ed.) (1955) *The Mind of Napoleon: A Selection from his Written and Spoken Words,* New York, Columbia University Press. A meaty and comprehensive collection.

Johnston, R.M. (ed.) (2002) *In the Words of Napoleon: The Emperor Day by Day,* London, Greenhill Books. A record compiled from Napoleon's writings.

Markham, J.D. (2003) *Imperial Glory: The Bulletins of Napoleon's 'Grand Armée',* London, Greenhill Books. A complete record of the military bulletins 1805–14, an important arm of Napoleon's propaganda.

## Secondary studies of Napoleon

Bainville, J. (1938) *Napoleon,* trans. H. Miles, London, Jonathan Cape (first published in French 1931). Still a classic, full of insights (but see Geyl below, pp.336–45, for a perceptive critique).

Ellis, G. (1997) *Napoleon,* Harlow, Longman. A scholarly, up-to-date critical analysis.

Ellis, G. (2003) *The Napoleonic Empire*, 2nd edn, London, Palgrave. Concise coverage incorporating scholarship up to 2003.

Fisher, H.A.L. (1971) *Napoleon*, Oxford, Oxford University Press (first published 1912). Despite its age, still a reliable, concise biography.

Geyl, P. (1965) *Napoleon: For and Against*, Harmondsworth, Penguin (first published 1949). A fascinating discussion of historians' verdicts on Napoleon.

Herold, J.C. (1991) *The Age of Napoleon*, Boston, Houghton Mifflin (first published 1963). Thoughtful coverage, well documented, unfortunately lacking references and bibliography.

Holtman, R.B. (1967) *The Napoleonic Revolution*, Philadelphia, J.B. Lippincott. Remains a good short thematic study analysing the main aspects of Napoleon's contribution.

Markham, F. (1963) *Napoleon*, London, Weidenfeld and Nicolson. Clear and reliable.

Rosebery, A.P.P., Earl of (1922) *Napoleon: The Last Phase*, London, Hodder (first published 1900). Remains an interesting study.

## Secondary studies of Stendhal and Staël

Caraccio, A. (1965) *Stendhal,* trans. D. Bayley, New York, New York University Press.

Herold, J.C. (1959) *Mistress to an Age: A Life of Madame de Staël*, London, Hamish Hamilton.

Villefosse, L. de and Bouissounouse, J. (1972) *The Scourge of the Eagle: Napoleon and the Liberal Opposition*, trans. and ed. M. Ross, London, Sidgwick and Jackson.

# Unit 9
# Napoleon and painting

*Prepared for the course team by Emma Barker*

# Contents

# Study components

| Weeks of study | Supplementary material | Audio-visual | Anthologies and set books |
|---|---|---|---|
| 1 | AV Notes<br>Illustrations Book | Video 2 | Anthology I |

# Objectives

By the end of your work on Unit 9 you should be able to:

- analyse paintings centred on the human figure in terms of how a work's form and content together produce its meaning;

- explain how and why French painting came to be used and controlled by the Napoleonic regime;

- discuss the problems of interpretation raised by Gros's Napoleonic paintings;

- locate Napoleonic painting within the broad shift from Neoclassicism to Romanticism in French art.

# 1   Introduction

If you visit the Louvre museum in Paris and choose the route leading to the Denon wing, you will find on the first floor two vast galleries, the Daru room and the Mollien room, devoted to late eighteenth- and early nineteenth-century French painting. Although they also contain many comparatively small works, notably portraits, these galleries are dominated by colossal pictures depicting historical and mythological subjects. Many of the images that we will be discussing in this unit belong to this genre. At the time, '**history painting**' (as it is generally known) constituted by far the most prestigious **genre of painting** for two principal reasons. First, it was considered to be far more demanding than the so-called lower genres (portraiture, landscape, still life, etc.): not only did the history painter have to work out a large-scale composition involving the human figure, but he was also expected to represent nature in its ideal forms rather than merely copying the familiar appearance of things, like artists who practised the lower genres.[31] Second, the subject matter of history paintings was considered to be much more significant than that of the lower genres, on account both of the exalted status of the gods and heroes who were depicted in them and of the elevating moral messages that they offered to the viewer. At least, this was the theory; the practice was often rather different, as we will see from considering examples produced during the Napoleonic era. This was increasingly to be the case as the nineteenth century progressed.

Most of the history paintings in the Daru and Mollien rooms have been in the Louvre, a royal palace that was turned into a museum in 1793, since the nineteenth century. Many of them were commissioned by the French state, which has a long tradition of promoting the arts for the sake of the personal glory of the ruler and the prestige of the nation as a whole. Many of the others were acquired by the state after being shown at the **Salon**, the public exhibition held at the Louvre every year or two during the eighteenth and early nineteenth centuries.[32] Works of art that had been commissioned by the state would also be exhibited in the Salon, so that the public could see the results of official patronage. Free entry attracted huge crowds and meant that the Salon audience was socially pretty diverse (see Figure 9.1). These institutional factors played a decisive role in shaping the very nature of French art during the eighteenth and early nineteenth centuries. The huge history paintings on

[31] The masculine pronoun is deliberate. It was extremely difficult for a woman to become a history painter because female students were not admitted to the Royal Academy of Painting and Sculpture, which taught the necessary skill in depicting the human figure. The core of its tuition was the life class, which involved drawing from the naked (male) model (see Unit 1, Figure 1.8, p.32). Women were excluded on grounds of modesty.

[32] The exhibition took its name from the room in which it was held, the *salon carré* in the Louvre.

display today in the Daru and Mollien rooms would not have come into existence without the state as actual patron or potential buyer: they are mostly too large to go anywhere but a museum or other public building. Moreover, the knowledge that his painting was going to be exhibited at the Salon meant that an artist would be conscious of the need for eye-catching effects in order to compete with all the other paintings hanging on the walls for the attention of the public. It is important to keep these points in mind when analysing French paintings of this period.

Between them, these galleries allow visitors to trace the chronological development of French painting from **Neoclassicism** (in the Daru room)

*Figure 9.1   Monsaldy and Devisme,* View of the Salon, *1799, engraving, Bibliothèque nationale de France, Paris.*

to Romanticism (in the Mollien room).[33] We can gain some sense of the changes involved by means of a comparison between a history painting by Jacques-Louis David (1748–1825), the principal exponent of Neoclassicism, and one by Eugène Delacroix (1798–1863), the leading French Romantic painter (whom you will study in more detail in Block 7). David's *Oath of the Horatii*, exhibited in the Salon of 1785 (see Plate 9.1 in the Illustrations Book), depicts an example of patriotic virtue from ancient Roman history with great clarity and simplicity. The statue-like figures stand out against a dark background, the setting is a plain box-like space, the colour range is limited and the paint surface smooth, almost photographic (though it should be noted that this effect is heightened by the fact that what you are looking at is, in fact, a photograph). By contrast, Delacroix's *Massacres of Chios*, exhibited in the Salon of 1824 (see Plate 9.2), depicts an episode from the Greek War of Independence, which was going on at the time. It has a vertical rather than a horizontal format, which means that the figures are crowded into a narrow foreground in a somewhat confusing way. Rather than being strong and heroic, like the main figures in David's painting, they are the helpless victims of Turkish oppression. Behind them, the open landscape appears very much as a flat backdrop. Despite its grim subject, the painting has a certain picturesque appeal, thanks to the exotic costumes, light tonality, vivid colours and loose handling of paint. Overall, it can be said that this work retains the ambitions of a history painting but breaks with the aesthetic and moral idealism traditionally expected of the genre.

A key figure in French painting between David and Delacroix is Antoine-Jean Gros (1771–1835), whose two most famous works, *Bonaparte Visiting the Plague-Stricken of Jaffa* (1804) and *Napoleon Visiting the Field of the Battle of Eylau* (1808), now hang in the Mollien room (Plates 9.15 and 9.19). A former pupil of David, Gros turned to the depiction of current political and military events in a lively, colouristic fashion in response to the propaganda demands of the Napoleonic regime. For Delacroix, Gros's work represented a dazzling achievement that he aspired to emulate, and, as a young man who came of age after the fall of the empire, he envied the older artist for having lived in an era of spectacular military exploits. In 1824 he wrote: 'the life of Napoleon is the epic of our century for all the arts' (Delacroix, 1938, p.78). *Jaffa* and *Eylau* continue to be admired today as pioneering examples of the Romantic style and, as such, are distinguished from most other Napoleonic propaganda painting, which seems conventional and uninspired by comparison. It has been argued that they 'enshrine not only Napoleon's heroism but also Gros's misgivings' and thus introduce 'an element of fundamental personal doubt' into French history painting

---

[33] Neoclassicism is the term applied to late-eighteenth and early-nineteenth century painting in the classical style. Such painting forms part of an existing tradition of classicizing painting which can be traced back to the Renaissance, but is distinguished from it by (among other things) a greater concern with archaeological correctness in the imitation of antique forms.

(Brookner, 1980, p.161), despite the fact that there exists no written evidence to suggest that the artist was at all disillusioned with Napoleon. Underlying this statement is the assumption that a great work of art must be the independent creation of an autonomous genius and cannot simply have been painted according to official dictates. This conception of artistic creation as self-expression in fact crystallized during the period that we are considering, and is one of the defining features of Romanticism as a broad cultural movement.

In this unit we will examine a range of Napoleonic imagery by David, Gros and a number of other artists, beginning with comparatively simple single-figure portraits and moving on to elaborate narrative compositions such as *Jaffa* and *Eylau*. In so doing, we will have three main aims:

1   To develop your skills of visual analysis and to demonstrate how a painting's form and content together produce its meaning. As part of this, we will seek to illuminate the broad cultural shift from the Enlightenment to Romanticism as it played out in Napoleonic painting.

2   To examine the relationship between art and politics. We will consider how painting came to be used and controlled by the Napoleonic regime for purposes of propaganda. As we will see, the fundamental problem driving Napoleonic propaganda was one of political legitimation: how to provide ideological justification for a leader who had seized power and whose rule rested ultimately on force.

3   To introduce you to some of the complex issues involved in interpreting works of art, with particular reference to Gros's best-known Napoleonic paintings. What makes it difficult to view *Jaffa* and *Eylau* as straightforwardly propagandist works is their depiction of suffering and death, which seems to evoke the costs rather than the benefits of Napoleon's rule. Rather than trying to account for the horrific elements in the paintings in terms of a hypothesis about the artist's intentions (that is, Gros's supposed doubts), we will relate them to the fundamental stresses and contradictions of the regime.

# 2   The portrait of Napoleon

## The general

Even early on, when he was a brilliant young general winning battles in Italy, Napoleon was already well aware of the value of images in promoting his career. It was not only owing to his own initiative that he had his portrait painted at this stage, but also because it was advantageous for an artist to be associated with a national hero. Gros, who had gone to Italy to pursue his studies as a history painter but found himself practising portraiture out of financial necessity, got himself introduced to Bonaparte's wife, Josephine, in 1796 'in the sole hope of getting to do the portrait of the general' (quoted in O'Brien, 1995, p.653). In the resulting painting, *General Bonaparte at the Bridge of Arcole* (1797), he is shown leading a charge across a bridge (see Plate 9.3). More famous than the actual painting, however, is the sketch for it, in which the loose brushwork enhances the overall dynamism of the image (see Plate 9.4). But even in the finished work there is a strong sense of movement that distinguishes it from the long-established tradition of military portraiture, which Gros took as his starting point, a tradition exemplified by Hyacinthe Rigaud's portraits of commanders (see Plate 9.5).

**EXERCISE**    Compare Gros's portrait of Bonaparte (Plate 9.3) to Rigaud's of a French marshal (Plate 9.5). In what ways does Gros follow the model provided by Rigaud, and how does he alter it in order to convey a greater sense of movement? Consider, in particular, the type of portrait (full-length, half-length, etc.), the setting of the scene and the sitter's pose.

**DISCUSSION**    Like Rigaud, Gros employs a three-quarter-length format, showing his sitter from just below the knees upwards, and with a battle going on in the background (though the battle is more implied than evident in the later work). However, the poses of each figure are very different. The marshal painted by Rigaud is not engaged in action but faces calmly frontwards, one hand resting on his sword hilt and the other gesturing towards the battle with his marshal's baton as a demonstration of his leadership. By contrast, Gros shows Bonaparte in the thick of battle, striding ahead while simultaneously looking back to rally his troops on. The twist in his body (torso facing to the right, head to the left) serves to animate the whole image. In addition, the waving flag that he holds aloft and his outstretched sword are both cut off at the edge of the picture, producing a sense that what we are seeing is a fleeting snapshot of an actual moment.

The overall result is a painting that is not a conventional portrait but has something of the character of a history painting, in so far as it depicts a decisive moment of military action. In fact, the event depicted by Gros was nothing of the kind since, although Bonaparte claimed to have successfully led a charge at Arcole, it actually took two more days' fighting before the French could cross the bridge. The story is typical of the way that Napoleon embroidered the truth for propaganda purposes throughout his career. His awareness of the value of good publicity is also evident from the fact that he paid to have Gros's portrait engraved (see Plate 9.6), thereby ensuring that it would reach a wide audience. The image that it conveys is of a brave commander who, by his example, inspires his men to follow him. Since he does not bother to look at the enemy, it is as if he knows his strategy in advance and is completely confident of victory. As such, he can be identified as a hero, a term which should be understood to mean a very particular kind of person who is certainly exceptional but perhaps not entirely admirable. This becomes apparent from the definition of 'hero' in the *Encyclopédie*, the great work of reference which embodies the rational, public-spirited and humanitarian ideals of the Enlightenment.

**EXERCISE**

Read the following passage from the *Encyclopédie* article 'Hero', considering what qualities identify the hero as opposed to the great man. Which type of man seems to owe more to innate talent and genius? Which type of man can be identified with enlightened ideals?

> A hero is defined as a man steadfast in difficulties, intrepid in peril and very valiant in combat; these qualities are linked more to temperament and to a certain configuration of the organs than to nobility of spirit. The great man is something very different – he joins the majority of moral virtues to talent and genius; he has only lofty and noble motives for his behaviour ... The title of *hero* depends upon success, that of the great man does not always depend upon it. His principle is virtue which is as unshakeable in prosperity as in misfortune.
>
> In short, humanity, gentleness and patriotism conjoined to talent constitute the virtues of the great man; bravura, courage, often temerity, knowledge of the art of war and military genius characterize to a greater extent the hero.
>
> (Quoted in Johnson, 1993, p.76)

**DISCUSSION**

The hero is above all a military figure; his principal quality is bravery in action, whereas the qualities of the great man are internal, moral ones. Whereas the qualities of the hero are part of his physical make-up and are simply what comes naturally to him, those of the great man seem to come from reflection and to provide him with a sense of direction. The hero is said to have military genius, which presumably means an innate instinct for what will work on the battlefield, while the great man is said to have moral virtues in addition to talent and genius. The implication seems to be that he has everything that the hero has and more – and also perhaps that he can claim more credit for his actions because they do not simply come naturally but require self-discipline, a striving after what is right.

The statement that the title of hero depends on success also suggests an element of chance and luck in the matter. By contrast, the great man is admirable because he sticks to his principles no matter what he goes through. Furthermore, since his virtues include 'humanity, gentleness and patriotism', it is clear that his superiority rests above all in his concern for other people. In this respect, as well as in his thoughtfulness, he can be seen to embody the ideals of the Enlightenment; as such, it is not surprising that the *Encyclopédie* should have presented him as more admirable. By comparison, the hero seems a rather problematic character, acting merely out of instinct and not obviously benefiting other people.

---

This text sheds light on the enlightened values that underlie neoclassical art and helps reveal the ways in which Napoleonic portraiture departs from them. In the later eighteenth century, the commemoration of great men came to be considered one of art's principal functions; the aim was to inspire the viewer to emulate their virtuous, patriotic spirit. From 1775 onwards, the arts administration of the monarchy commissioned a series of statues of the great men of France, which only came to a halt with the Revolution. The cult of the great man culminated in the Revolution with the creation of the Pantheon in 1791.[34] Among those subsequently buried there was the revolutionary journalist Marat, assassinated in 1793, whom David commemorated shortly afterwards in a famous painting; it can be seen to embody the enlightened ideal of the great man, whose virtuous life found its culmination in a noble death (see Plate 9.7). David shows Marat at the moment of his death, slumped back in the bath in which he sat to soothe a skin disease, his pen still in his hand. The closed eyes, the light falling from above, the simple composition made up largely of horizontal and vertical lines, and the empty space above the figure together create a mood of great serenity, which implies that, just as he served his country in life with his pen, so he is glad to die for it. That Marat was a truly enlightened great man, humane as well as patriotic, is indicated by the note on the box that he has frugally been using as a table; it is a request for charity to a widow and her children, suggesting that he is a father to the poor. (In fact, Marat was a deeply controversial political figure, as widely reviled as revered.)

As a posthumous portrait of a civilian, David's *The Death of Marat* is a very different type of image from Gros's *Bonaparte at Arcole*, which serves to promote the military career of a man who was not only very much alive but even (so the image suggests) invincible. Nevertheless, the contrast between the two paintings can help to elucidate the distinctive features of the Napoleonic image. First, whereas David universalizes his scene by depicting Marat naked and idealizing his notorious ugly face and diseased body – thereby turning him into a timeless, almost classical figure – the uniform and flag in Gros's painting locate the scene in a particular time and place. Bonaparte is thus identified as a modern

[34] See Block 1, Unit 6, p.212.

figure, a specifically French hero. Moreover, whereas David's painting is above all a rational image, providing the viewer with evidence of the qualities which made Marat admirable, Gros's is an irrational one, seeking not to persuade or instruct but rather to overwhelm the viewer with the glamour of Bonaparte's appearance and the force of his personality.[35] In it, traditional military heroism can be seen to dissolve into 'an essentially modern notion of personal charisma' (Prendergast, 1997, pp.122, 148). In describing the painting in these terms, there is a danger of projecting back on to this early portrait the fully-fledged Napoleonic legend of later years. However, it also helps to distinguish this portrayal from those produced once Napoleon had embarked on a political career. As we will see, the image that he cultivated as ruler shifted away from the personal qualities of the hero towards the moral virtues of the great man. In general terms, it represents a compromise between the values of the Enlightenment (rationalism, humanity, etc.) and Romantic concerns (notably, in its emphasis on the quasi-magical 'genius' of the unique individual).[36]

## The First Consul

Let us now consider another relatively early portrait, David's *Bonaparte Crossing the Alps*, in which the then First Consul is shown at the Great Saint Bernard at the start of the campaign which led to the defeat of the Austrians at Marengo in June 1800 (see Plate 9.8). As you learned from the previous units, Bonaparte actually crossed the Alps on a humble mule rather than on the splendid mount depicted in this painting. What interests me, however, is not so much the falsity of this propaganda image but exactly how it served Napoleon's ambitions. In fact, the painting originated as a commission from the King of Spain for a gallery of famous military leaders, but a copy was immediately ordered by Bonaparte himself (this is the version illustrated here). He had previously sat for his portrait to David, apparently at the artist's own request, on his return from his first Italian campaign in 1797, but that painting was never completed. David is supposed to have been greatly inspired by the encounter, exclaiming (according to one of his pupils, writing years later): 'O my friends, what a fine head he has! It's pure, it's great, it's as beautiful as the Antique! Here is a man to whom altars would have been erected in ancient times ... Bonaparte is my hero!' (Delécluze, 1983, p.200; quoted in Brooker, 1980, p.142). In 1800, however, he was granted no sittings by Napoleon, who is reported to have declared:

[35] Some art historians have argued that David evokes traditional Christian imagery, notably depictions of the dead Christ; against this type of interpretation, it should be noted that the painting contains no hint of any supernatural element, no suggestion (for example) that Marat is going to be wafted up to heaven.

[36] See the discussion of Napoleon's 'charisma' and 'genius' in Units 7–8, pp.51–3.

Likeness is not produced by an exact reproduction of features, by a pimple on the nose. What the painter must show is the character of the face, the thing that makes it alive ... Nobody wants to know if the portraits of great men look like them. It is enough that their genius lives in them.

(Delécluze, 1983, p.232)

This statement at once draws on the classical tradition of idealized representation (such as we have seen in David's *Marat*) and expresses a typically Napoleonic faith in the charisma of the heroic leader. Whether or not he actually uttered these words, Napoleon undoubtedly did have an aversion to sitting for his portrait. Nor did this present too great a problem in the case of official portraits, the purpose of which was not simply to record an individual likeness but also to embody the authority of the office (as king, general, minister, etc.). Certainly, when David put the two versions of the portrait on show in the Louvre in 1801, none of the critics seemed bothered by the acknowledged lack of resemblance. This can be attributed to the fact that it was, in effect, an official portrait (even if it had not initially been commissioned by the regime), and also to its significance as a work of art in its own right, as an ambitious painting by the most famous French artist of the day. The fact that David put them on display (though not in fact in the Salon) is also significant; it suggests that he saw himself as painting as much for the Parisian public as for the person who commissioned the painting.

**EXERCISE**   Compare *Bonaparte Crossing the Alps* (Plate 9.8) to *Bonaparte at the Bridge of Arcole* (Plate 9.3). In each case, consider the size of the painting (check the measurements in the caption), the type of portrait (is the figure shown full-length, for example?), the relative importance of the background, how the figure relates (or doesn't relate) to the viewer outside the painting, whether or not a sense of movement is conveyed, the brushwork (highly finished or loose and sketchy?). For the moment, we will concentrate on these **formal** properties and leave aside broader questions of meaning.

**DISCUSSION**   David's painting is quite a bit larger than Gros's, a more modest three-quarter-length portrait. Also, whereas *Bonaparte Crossing the Alps* includes craggy mountains and a windswept sky, *Bonaparte at the Bridge of Arcole* has only a hazy background, which can just be glimpsed behind the figure. Whereas, in the latter painting, Bonaparte's gaze is directed towards his soldiers, somewhere within the imaginary space that extends beyond the picture frame, David shows him looking outwards towards the viewer. Moreover, although the figure's upward-gesturing arm can be read as an instruction to his soldiers, its exaggerated drama suggests that it is really directed towards the viewer outside the picture. It is as if he is inviting the viewer to follow him. Also, his equestrian pose means that he looks down on everyone (soldiers and viewers alike) from a great height, whereas Gros's figure is roughly on a level with his men. Rather than sharing the dynamism of the earlier painting, David's has a strangely frozen quality, despite depicting energetic action. The rearing horse has a sculptural stillness and Napoleon's idealized features are impassive. This effect is reinforced by the smoothness of the highly finished manner used for the equestrian group, which contrasts with Gros's looser, livelier handling.

The question then arises: how do we account for these differences? Clearly, we are dealing with two painters each with his own style, but this provides only part of the answer. The larger size of *Bonaparte Crossing the Alps* and the grand equestrian format (often used for monarchs) can be related to the fact that, by 1800, Napoleon was no longer a mere general but had become the nation's leader. A crucial clue towards the painting's meaning is provided by the names inscribed on the rocks in the bottom-left foreground: Napoleon, Hannibal, Karolus Magnus (Charlemagne), thereby identifying Bonaparte with great military leaders who had crossed the Alps before him. Together with the way that he seems to be inviting the viewer to follow him onwards and upwards, they give a mythic dimension to the image. He is presented not simply as a hero but as a man of destiny, who will lead his army to military victory and, by implication, the French people to a glorious future. In this respect, it is important to note the tricolour flag being carried by the artillery men struggling up the mountainside; it identifies them with the nation, just as Napoleon appears here less as an individual than as the embodiment of military glory. It could also be argued that, by showing him calmly riding a fiery horse and defying the wild nature behind him, the painting implies he is capable of controlling a chaotic political situation and establishing a new order that will safeguard the gains of the Revolution. As such, it can be seen to justify the authority he had seized and thus to function as propaganda for the regime. While any official portrait is, in some sense, a form of propaganda, the Napoleonic crisis of legitimation meant that images of the new ruler had to (as it were) 'work' that much harder.

**EXERCISE**   Now look at Gros's *Bonaparte as First Consul* of 1802 (see Plate 9.9). How does it differ from the previous portraits of Napoleon we have looked at? What kind of claims does it make on his behalf? Consider the portrait type, setting, pose (including gesture and direction of gaze), costume and accessories.

Note: the uppermost paper on the table is headed by the word *traités* (treaties) followed by a list of names, concluding with 'Amiens'; below this are three further entries, which read '18 Brumaire', 'Concordat', 'Comices de Lyon'.[37]

**DISCUSSION**  This is the first full-length standing portrait we have looked at, and, for the first time, we see Bonaparte in an interior setting, which gives the image a more civilian character than the previous portraits where he is shown first and foremost as a military leader. He is still wearing a uniform and a sword, but the uniform is richly embroidered and seems more ceremonial than functional. At the same time, the plain backdrop counteracts the opulence of his attire and that of the fringed tablecloth, and means that the overall effect is still quite austere. In this respect, it is also significant that his hair is severely short rather than long and flowing as in Gros's previous portrait of Bonaparte. Rather than gesturing commandingly, he points towards the pile of papers on the table; the writing on the top document serves to emphasize not his military victories but rather his achievements as a statesman and a peacemaker. He is not staring out at the viewer but instead looks towards the right and seems to be listening or thinking. The image insists not so much on Napoleon's glorious destiny as on his executive role as head of government and the benefits of his rule.

This portrait established the standard image of Bonaparte as First Consul; it served as the model for several further portraits commissioned from Gros and other artists, usually to hang in public buildings in provincial cities to serve as a focus of loyalty. Prior to 1802, he had continued to be portrayed above all as a military leader (as in David's portrait) rather than in his official capacity. The reason for the delay in establishing the official image for the First Consul was presumably that nobody had any clear idea of what such an image should look like, given that the office had just been invented and was inherently ambiguous. On the one hand, the title of consul was derived from republican Rome while, on the other, the constitution gave the First Consul quasi-monarchical powers. It was during the consulate that Napoleon adopted the antique-style cropped haircut, which was said at the time to make him resemble the Roman consul Brutus, whose appearance was recorded in a famous bust (see Figure 9.2 and Figures 7.1 and 7.12, pp.17, 66). The flattering (and also hopeful) implication of the comparison was that he, like his ancient predecessor, was a man of integrity, devoted to the good of the republic, and not one to bring about a return to monarchical rule. Gros's painting not only records Bonaparte's new haircut, but also embodies the tensions of the position of First Consul in the way that it tempers official

[37] The Treaty of Amiens established a (temporary) peace with England in 1802; the Comices de Lyon was the election of Bonaparte as president of the Cisalpine Republic (northern Italy, effectively) in the same year.

*Figure 9.2   Anonymous,* Head of Lucius Junius Brutus, *bronze, Musei Capitolini, Rome. Photo: Scala.*

splendour with a certain austerity and in its emphasis on function rather than ceremony, in keeping with the spirit of the Revolution.

## The emperor

With Napoleon's coronation as emperor in 1804, a new type of official image was once again required. Portraits of the emperor in his ceremonial robes were commissioned from several established artists; these all revived a traditional type of royal portraiture from the eighteenth century. The example shown in the Illustrations Book is by a former David student, François Gérard (1770–1837), by now a fashionable portrait painter (see Plate 9.10). A portrait of Napoleon as emperor was also painted by a former David student of a younger generation, Jean-Auguste-Dominique Ingres (1780–1867), apparently on his own initiative. When *Napoleon on the Imperial Throne* (see Plate 9.11) was exhibited at the Salon of 1806, the catalogue stated that it belonged to the Legislative Body, but documentary evidence indicates that it had been purchased from the artist rather than having originated as a commission. Ingres had previously received a commission for a portrait of the First Consul for the city of Liège, and must have been disappointed that he had not been given the opportunity to exhibit the painting, which commemorates Napoleon signing a decree ordering the reconstruction of an area of the city that had been bombarded by Austrian troops (see Plate 9.12). He may, therefore, have come up with the idea of painting a portrait of the emperor 'on spec' in order to attract attention and win acclaim. If so, the gamble did not entirely pay off; although Ingres did succeed in selling the picture, the critical reception was almost unrelievedly hostile. The question that concerns us is: why?

**EXERCISE**

Compare Ingres's *Napoleon on the Imperial Throne* (Plate 9.11) to Gérard's portrait of the emperor (Plate 9.10), thinking about the difference in the effect conveyed. Consider the pose and, in particular, the way the figure relates to the viewer of the painting. How much sense of three-dimensional space do you get from each work? How much emphasis is given in each case to the ceremonial robes and imperial regalia?

**DISCUSSION**

The most basic difference is indicated by the title of Ingres's painting, which depicts Napoleon seated on a throne, whereas Gérard's is a full-length standing portrait. Also, whereas the latter work shows the emperor's body at a slight angle to the front of the picture space and his head turned slightly to face the viewer, Ingres shows Napoleon in a strictly frontal pose facing the viewer head-on. The image is not strictly symmetrical but almost so, with the two sceptres balancing each other on either side of the figure. The effect is strangely stiff and formal by comparison with Gérard's imposing but more natural-seeming image. The head-on pose used by Ingres also produces an impression of flatness: Napoleon is set slightly back from the front of the picture, distancing him from the viewer, but the figure seems rather two-dimensional, partly because of the way it is so swathed in robes that there is little sense of a body underneath them. Also, because the enthroned figure takes up most of the picture surface, allowing for only a hint of dark backdrop without much detail, there is very little sense of any depth to the scene. The effect is rather claustrophobic by comparison with Gérard's painting, in which the figure is set in a larger space, with the throne behind it and a stool to one side. The stool also provides a resting place for an orb and sceptre, so that the figure does not seem overloaded with regalia as he does in Ingres's painting, where he not only holds both sceptres but also has a ceremonial sword under his arm. Similarly, whereas in Gérard's painting Napoleon's chain gets lost in the ermine, it is completely visible in Ingres's painting where it forms a flat semi-circle that echoes other circular shapes around his face, such as the laurel leaf crown.

In fact, *Napoleon on his Imperial Throne* is crammed with traditional symbols of power. The sceptre surmounted by a statuette, the other sceptre (the 'hand of justice') and the sword all had associations with Charlemagne. In the run-up to the coronation, the regime had adopted as official propaganda the flattering notion of Napoleon as a modern Charlemagne (which was already current, as we have seen from David's portrait). Much effort was expended on legitimating his imperial authority by linking him to the last emperor to unite western Europe under his rule. The hand of justice, which had supposedly belonged to Charlemagne, was in fact fabricated for Napoleon's coronation. The great advantage of the early medieval monarchs as a source of legitimation was their remoteness from the Bourbon dynasty deposed by the Revolution. Another Carolingian[38] (and ancient Roman) symbol of power appropriated by Napoleon was the imperial eagle, which appears carved on to the throne and woven into the carpet in Ingres's painting. The eagle was originally an attribute of Jupiter, the king of the gods in classical mythology, and Ingres may have based Napoleon's pose on an image of the god which itself derived ultimately from a famous lost statue, known as the Olympian Jupiter, by the ancient Greek sculptor Phidias (see Figure 9.3). However, the pose could have come from any number of ancient or medieval depictions of enthroned figures. The crucial point is that it symbolized divine power and, when used for an earthly ruler, signified a divine right to rule.

When the painting was exhibited at the Salon, the main complaint was that it looked 'gothic': that is, medieval (Siegfried, 1980, pp.70–1). More than one critic compared it to the work of the Flemish painter Jan van Eyck (d.1441), whose famous Ghent altarpiece was one of the looted trophies of war then on display in the Louvre; the central panel of God enthroned could in fact have been a source for the emperor's pose (see Figure 9.4). What elicited the comparison was the stiffness of the pose, meticulous attention to detail, and bright but restricted colour scheme (red, gold and white, essentially). Commentators also objected to the way that the figure is so loaded with drapery and ornament that it lacks any sense of physical presence: 'the head seems to have been set on cushions', complained one (quoted in Shelton, 1999, p.500). Several were reminded of images of medieval kings and cult statues of the madonna. These comments suggest that it was not simply the 'barbarous' style that aroused concern but also, for some at least, the religious character of the image and the vision of kingship it embodied. The claim that Napoleon was a ruler by divine right alienated all those who had rallied to him as the saviour of the Revolution and who considered that his legitimacy derived not from God but from the people. By 1806 the regime had realized its mistake and had moved away from the medieval symbolism

---

[38] The Frankish dynasty founded by Charlemagne (d.814).

*Figure 9.3  Comte de Caylus,* Jupiter, *1752–67, engraving, 8.3 × 5.6 cm, Bibliothèque nationale de France, Paris.*

used at the time of the coronation; a plan of 1803 for a statue of Charlemagne to be erected in a prominent site in Paris had been abandoned.[39] Ingres was thus out-of-step with official propaganda imagery.

The failure of Ingres's painting is revealing of the problems of political legitimation faced by the regime. If it was difficult to justify the authority of a ruler who had seized power, it was even harder to justify a monarchy based on usurpation (the authority Napoleon had usurped being either that of the Bourbon dynasty from a royalist point of view or that of the people from a republican one). Ingres's image of timeless, otherworldly majesty can thus be seen as compensating, or rather trying to compensate, for the all too recent and highly dubious origins of Napoleon's imperial rule. Its failure was not simply a matter of bad timing but, on a deeper level, bound up with the opportunistic,

[39] This did not mean that the regime abandoned the claim that Napoleon ruled by divine right: see Units 7–8, pp.68–9.

*Figure 9.4   Jan van Eyck,* Christ of the Mystic Lamb, *detail of the Ghent alterpiece, 1426, oil and tempera on wood, 208 × 79 cm, St Bavo Cathedral, Ghent. Photo: © Paul M.R. Maeyaert.*

improvisatory response to the problem on the part of the regime, which seized at any and every identity (Charlemagne, Brutus, etc.) that could serve a propaganda purpose and cast them aside as soon as they lost their relevance and usefulness. Furthermore, while it was not bothered about the overall consistency and coherence of its propaganda, the need to appeal to different shades of political opinion meant that the image of the emperor would ideally balance contradictory elements, reconciling sacred and secular, monarchical and revolutionary, traditional and modern, irrational and rational. The problem with Ingres's painting was that it focused exclusively on one side of the equation; the same can be said of David's *Napoleon in his Study* of 1812 (see Plate 9.13), which otherwise could hardly offer a more different image of Napoleon.

**EXERCISE**  Which of the previous portraits we have looked at does *Napoleon in his Study* most closely resemble, and in what ways does it depart from this model? What kinds of claims does David make here on Napoleon's behalf, and how do they differ from those made by Ingres's portrait of Napoleon enthroned?

Note: the word 'Code' that appears on the document on the desk indicates that it is a copy of the Civil Code or Code Napoléon of 1804. In considering the significance of this image, you may find it helpful to look back at what is said about the Civil Code in Units 7–8, pp.54–8.

**DISCUSSION**  This painting returns to the **iconography**[40] of Napoleon as First Consul, showing him standing in an interior in close proximity to official papers. More precisely, the portrait refers back to the period of the consulate, during which the Civil Code was drawn up, though it shows him stout and balding as he would have appeared in 1812. If anything, the image is more sober and businesslike than Gros's 1802 portrait, since Napoleon is wearing a relatively plain military uniform rather than an opulent ceremonial one. Also, since the papers are lying not on a table but on a desk at which he has evidently been working, there is an even stronger emphasis on his executive role. The clock giving the time as 4.15 and the guttering candles indicate that he has been working through the night. Another contrast with the consular portrait is that Napoleon is looking out at the viewer; this, combined with the fact that he is standing in close proximity to us rather than staring down from a great height, makes him seem more human and accessible to the viewer who, as we saw earlier, can be identified with the French people (see p.110 above). Thus, instead of an all-powerful and unapproachable monarch ruling by divine right, such as Ingres depicted, here we have the ruler as enlightened bureaucrat who labours on behalf of 'us', his people.

Like Ingres's painting, David's portrait of Napoleon in his study does not simply offer a certain image of the emperor but is bound up with a broader crisis of political legitimation. It acknowledges that, without a

[40] The study of the meanings of images. In art history the term is generally used to designate an approach that seeks to decode meaning through an attention to symbolism, etc. However, it can involve a consideration of formal features as well as subject matter. As applied to portraiture, it traditionally meant a list or catalogue of all the images of a particular person.

sacred basis for its authority, power has to keep working to justify itself. A ruler who lacks divine right is judged on his performance. In this respect, the problems faced by Napoleon were only an extreme version of those that the Enlightenment critique of established authority posed for more venerable monarchies. They, too, now needed to justify themselves in rational, utilitarian terms, on the basis of the benefits they brought their subjects. It is also important to note that *Napoleon in his Study* was another unofficial portrait, having been commissioned by a Scottish admirer, Alexander Douglas, the future Duke of Hamilton. Just as Ingres overcompensated for the instability of the regime, so David's modern, rational and functional image went too far in the opposite direction to be effective as imperial propaganda. Despite presenting an entirely positive vision of Napoleon (not least in showing him conscientiously labouring on the Civil Code by himself, when in fact his contribution largely took the form of chairing a legislative committee), it lacked the mystique and glamour needed to capture the popular imagination. Its sobriety stands in marked contrast to the propaganda images of the emperor commissioned by the imperial administration.

---

**EXERCISE**    You should now watch *Women and Portraiture in Napoleonic Europe* (Video 2, band 2), referring first to the AV Notes.

---

# 3   Gros and the Napoleonic propaganda machine

Although portraits of Napoleon were manufactured on a large scale and widely distributed, they could only act as propaganda for the regime up to a certain point. Given the institutional circumstances sketched out in the introduction to this unit, the most effective way to use art as propaganda was with large-scale history paintings that would attract the attention and excite the interest of a large audience when they were exhibited in the Salon. State patronage for such painting was revived on a lavish scale under Napoleon, a development that was very welcome to artists after the lean years of the Revolution, during which very few works were commissioned by the government. However, Napoleonic patronage was also characterized by a much tighter control over the form and content of history painting than had previously been the case, in order to ensure that the resulting works fulfilled the propaganda objectives of the regime. The works in question were, above all, paintings of military subjects. Just as French men were conscripted en masse into the army, so French painters were enlisted in the service of the empire to celebrate the battles the soldiers fought: in 1811 a critic described David, Gros and other leading artists as 'the generals of painting' (quoted in Wrigley, 1993, p.337). French art was thus subjected to the control of a propaganda machine, paralleling the strict censorship and surveillance imposed on every other form of expression.

These shifts in French painting were heralded quite soon after Bonaparte seized power; in a letter of 1800 he wrote to his brother Lucien, the minister of the interior, listing six battles that he wanted to have depicted and asking him to select appropriate painters for the task. One of them was the battle of Marengo, while the others were all drawn from his Egyptian (in fact, Middle Eastern) campaign of 1798–9, despite the fact it had ended in failure. From the first, therefore, not only did the regime turn to military painting for purposes of propaganda, but it is also evident that a certain sleight of hand was involved; that is to say, the Napoleonic strategy was not to pretend that a setback had never occurred, but boldly to present even a disaster as a triumph. This holds especially true of the two paintings that we will be focusing on here: Gros's *Jaffa*, which deals with the most inglorious episode of the entire Egyptian campaign, and *Eylau*, which depicts a problematic episode from a later campaign. Two points need to be made in advance. First, both paintings rely on a notion of France's 'civilizing mission', in which enlightened ideals are harnessed to a new nationalistic and also colonialist agenda. Second, both also testify to the limitations of Napoleon's strict censorship laws, since it was precisely because news of what had really happened was circulating in France that the regime found it necessary to promote its own version of events. (We will come back to both points.)

## *Bonaparte Visiting the Plague-Stricken of Jaffa*

First and foremost, *Jaffa* (like *Eylau*) contributed to the personality cult of Napoleon, which formed the core of the regime's propaganda. In this respect, however, it is important to note that this painting, exhibited in the Salon of 1804, was actually one of the first military scenes commissioned by the regime to exalt Napoleon in this way. This was largely because it took some time before the propaganda machine needed to organize a large-scale system of official patronage was in place. After Bonaparte seized power, David hoped to be given responsibility for running government art policy himself; in 1800 he was offered the title of 'painter to the government' but turned it down, apparently because it lacked the powers that he wanted. It was not until the end of 1802 that the administrator who was to be in charge of running the system was appointed; he was Dominique-Vivant Denon (1747–1825) and the new post that he filled was director general of the Musée Napoléon (as the museum in the Louvre was known at that time; the wing of the Louvre in which French paintings of this period now hang is named after Denon). Although a number of military paintings were commissioned in an ad hoc fashion during the consulate (including *Jaffa*), it was only during the empire that propaganda art was produced on a large scale.

To start with, moreover, military painting did not necessarily glorify Napoleon himself. When this genre was revived around 1800 after a long period in which paintings of battles were relatively uncommon, it was primarily in order to celebrate the bravery of all ranks of the French army, common soldiers as well as officers. Just days after the battle of Nazareth was fought in 1799, Bonaparte announced a competition for a painting to commemorate the event, one of the few successes of his Egyptian campaign, which he claimed as a great victory; it was not a personal triumph, however, since the French troops had been led on this occasion by another general. When the competition eventually took place in 1801, the government provided the artists with a summary account of the battle, singling out a number of individual acts of courage. The oil sketches submitted as competition entries were exhibited in the Louvre; the winner was Gros, who had made careful use of the documentation provided (see Plate 9.14). What is striking about his sketch is, on the one hand, its immediacy and dynamism and, on the other, its lack of a single focus of interest. The composition consists, as you might expect from the brief, of numerous distinct groups of figures; the French commander, General Junot (on a white horse), does not dominate the scene but is set well back. A number of critics at the time objected to this lack of dramatic unity, which transgressed the hierarchical conventions of traditional history painting, in which the centre of attention is the most important person in the scene.

Significantly, the commission was subsequently cancelled; Gros never worked up his sketch of *The Battle of Nazareth* into the vast painting, some 7.6 metres (25 feet) wide, decreed by the terms of the competition. Although there may well have been other reasons, the decision must have been largely determined by the increasingly exclusive propaganda cult of Napoleon. The painting Gros produced instead, *Bonaparte Visiting the Plague-Stricken of Jaffa* (see Plate 9.15), testifies to the authoritarian nature of the new regime on a number of levels. For one thing, it was not commissioned by means of the democratic system of the competition, which had become the standard method of distributing official patronage during the Revolution. Instead, it was commissioned on Bonaparte's own initiative, apparently without even consulting Denon. Arguably, moreover, whereas Gros's composition for *The Battle of Nazareth* has a democratic structure that accords with the republican ideals of the Revolution, *Jaffa* adopts the hierarchic structure of traditional history painting (as noted in the previous paragraph).

---

**EXERCISE**      Compare *Jaffa* (Plate 9.15) to *The Battle of Nazareth* (Plate 9.14), thinking about the ways in which the composition of the former conforms to the traditional model of history painting. How might you see it as less democratic, more authoritarian? Bear in mind not only relationships between the figures within the painting but also your relationship, as viewer, to the picture.

**DISCUSSION**     Instead of giving equal attention to soldiers of different ranks and making it hard to work out who exactly is the commanding officer, as he did in *The Battle of Nazareth*, Gros places the most important figure, Bonaparte, in the centre of the scene in accordance with the traditions of history painting. Also, since the figure scale is much larger in *Jaffa*, Bonaparte takes up proportionally more of the picture than any of the figures in *The Battle of Nazareth*. He wears a splendid uniform which makes him stand out from the other figures, most of whom are either dressed in flowing robes or naked. He is the focus of attention, both for the figures in the painting, several of whom turn to look at him, and for us, the viewers, whose gaze is directed towards him; he is a commanding figure in every sense of the phrase. By comparison, *The Battle of Nazareth* is more democratic not simply in terms of equalizing soldiers of different ranks but also in allowing the viewer's eye to wander over it freely.

When *Jaffa* was exhibited in 1804, it was greeted with great acclaim and would thus seem to have fulfilled the propaganda purpose for which it was intended. Like *The Battle of Nazareth*, it deals with the later stages of the Egyptian campaign after the French had invaded Syria, which, like Egypt, formed part of the Ottoman (Turkish) empire. The French assault on Jaffa in March 1799 culminated in the massacre on Bonaparte's orders of some 2,500–3,000 Turks, who had surrendered the garrison in return for a promise that their lives would be spared. It also involved the rape and slaughter of many civilians. Such actions flatly contradicted the avowed purpose of the campaign, which was justified on the grounds that it was not so much a conquest as a liberation that would bring enlightenment to the benighted lands of the East. In order to back up this conception of a 'civilizing mission', Bonaparte brought large numbers of scholars, scientists and artists with him to Egypt. French soldiers not only carried out atrocities at Jaffa, however, but were also themselves struck down in large numbers by the plague there. On his retreat to Cairo, two months later, Bonaparte gave orders for those still alive to be poisoned so as to avoid having to evacuate them.[41] It was this incident that was the most shocking from a contemporary European point of view, and the story rapidly gained currency in the British press (see Figure 9.5), some of the victims having survived to tell it to the British, who entered Jaffa after the French left. It also reached France, and it was

[41] For a defence of Napoleon's actions, see Stendhal, LN, pp.41–2. Stendhal mistakenly locates the poisoning in Acre.

clearly in order to counter these rumours that Gros was commissioned to paint his picture. *Jaffa* thus had a very specific propagandist function.

The painting depicts a visit made by Bonaparte in March 1799 to some of the plague-stricken French soldiers in a hospital in Jaffa. The catalogue of the 1804 Salon describes it as follows:

> Bonaparte, general in chief of the army of the Orient, at the moment when he touched a pestilential tumour while visiting the hospital at Jaffa ... To further distance the frightening idea of a sudden and incurable contagion, he had opened before him some pestilential tumours and touched several. He gave, by this magnanimous devotion, the first example of a genre of courage unknown until then and which has since had imitators.

(Quoted in Grigsby, 1995, p.9)

Bonaparte apparently did insist on the non-contagiousness of the disease, and according to his chief medical officer Desgenettes (who stands in the painting between Bonaparte and the sick man he is touching), he did have some physical contact with the plague-stricken during his visit. The precise subject seems to have been devised by Gros in consultation with Denon.

POISONING THE SICK AT JAFFA.

*Figure 9.5   George Cruikshank,* Napoleon Poisoning the Sick at Jaffa, *illustration from William Combe,* The Life of Napoleon, *1817, from the copy in the William Henry Hoyt Collection, Rare Book Collection, University of North Carolina at Chapel Hill.*

**EXERCISE**    Now look at the painting (Plate 9.15) and consider the following
questions:

1   How does the image of Bonaparte that it offers serve to counter the
    accusations made against him? How might his action be seen (in the
    light of the catalogue entry) to embody enlightened ideals?

2   How does Gros evoke the horrors of the plague? How might this
    contribute to the propagandist function of the painting?

3   How does Gros evoke the Middle Eastern setting? How might this
    contribute to the propagandist function of the painting?

**DISCUSSION**   1   Completely ignoring the crimes that could be attributed to Bonaparte,
    both massacres and poisonings, the painting depicts him as calm and
    fearless in face of a terrible disease. His composure is heightened by
    contrast with the men on either side of him, one of whom covers his
    face with a handkerchief while the one kneeling on the right seems
    to want to protect him from infection. He is shown not as a ruthless
    tyrant capable of having his own men murdered, but rather as a
    compassionate leader willing to risk his own life for their well-being.
    He also embodies enlightened values since he touches one of the
    plague boils with the aim of dispelling a supposedly unfounded and
    thus irrational fear of contagion.

2   The plague-stricken are mostly naked and slumped on the ground in
    poses expressive of mental and physical anguish (cowering in a
    corner, tearing their hair, desperately reaching out, etc.). They are
    also enveloped in shadow, as if to suggest that what they are going
    through is too horrific to be shown in the clear light of day; their
    blood-shot eyes stare out crazily through the darkness, and the
    blankets in which they are wrapped look rather like shrouds. The
    painting thus acknowledges that horrific suffering did take place and
    that French soldiers were among the victims, but attributes this
    suffering to a horrific natural cause, the plague, rather than French
    brutality or any other wrongdoing. This contributes to the
    propagandist function of the painting, as does the macabre
    fascination of the scene, which similarly distracts attention from the
    question of pinning down the blame.

3   The architectural setting, with its pointed arches, elaborate
    crenellations and tall minaret, is indicative of a Middle Eastern
    setting, as too are the turbans and flowing robes of the Arab figures.
    The warm, golden light and extensive use of red also serve to evoke
    a sultry, intense atmosphere that might be regarded as typically
    eastern. The overall sense of a mysterious, exotic place adds to the
    fascination of the composition and thus, like the plague horrors,
    enhances its propaganda function by side-stepping more mundane
    issues of accountability. In so far as the plague itself might be seen as

a specifically eastern phenomenon, it is further implied that no Frenchman can have played any part in causing this suffering. Since the tricolour can be seen flying from the top of the city, the painting also appeals to patriotic pride in French victories and thus endorses a colonialist agenda, while also conveniently skirting round the fact that the French did not hold Jaffa.

---

What is paradoxical about this painting is that, while Bonaparte is ostensibly presented here as the exponent of rational values, the impression that it conveys is not so much of a modern secular leader as of a saviour in the Christian tradition. His hand extended towards one of the plague-stricken suggests that he has miraculous powers of healing. As one of Gros's fellow artists put it, in an ode to the painting: 'the hero can cure at a glance' (quoted in Porterfield, 1998, p.56). It thus effectively attributes to Napoleon something very like 'the king's touch', the miraculous power to heal scrofulous abscesses attributed to French monarchs since the Middle Ages. The only problem with such an interpretation is that it is a bit too neat and fails to account for the sheer abundance of religious allusions. Napoleon might also be compared to St Roch, the patron saint of plague sufferers, or even to Christ.[42] The composition, with its colonnades, recalls paintings of Christ healing the paralytic at the pool of Bethesda (see Figure 9.6); there is even a blind man groping his way forward at the right as if hoping for a miraculous cure. Nor do the religious resonances stop here; the naked figures of the plague-stricken resemble the damned in hell, cut off as they are from the radiant light around the Christ-like leader. In fact, the figure seated at the left is based on one of the damned in Michelangelo's *Last Judgement* in the Sistine Chapel (see Figure 9.7).

Gros's painting is thus positively overloaded with allusions to religious images, in much the way that Ingres's portrait of Napoleon enthroned is crammed with symbols of divine power. Despite the differences of style and genre between these works, both testify in this respect to the problem of embodying authority in an iconography drawn from the art of the past (that is, a standard repertoire of stock poses, motifs, symbols, etc.) in a post-revolutionary culture in which the equivalence of monarchical and Christian power had collapsed. In consequence, the meanings of iconography had become unfixed. Thus, Napoleon could be depicted as a sacred monarch, but there was no guarantee that viewers would take the image in the spirit in which it was intended; it would be

---

[42] Given that this work dates from after Napoleon had made the Concordat with the Church, it is safe to assume that these religious references are intended to convey a specifically Christian meaning. In this respect, Gros's use of traditional religious imagery differs fundamentally from that in David's painting of Marat. In the latter case, the artist cannot have intended to identify Marat with Christ, in view of the Jacobins' replacement of Christianity with deism as the official religion.

*Figure 9.6 Bartolomé Esteban Murillo,* Christ Healing the Paralytic at the Pool of Bethesda, *1668, oil on canvas, 237 x 261 cm, National Gallery, London. Photo: © The National Gallery, London.*

likely, for example, to strike a royalist as blasphemous. However, it is also important to note a fundamental difference in approach between Gros and Ingres. The latter uses iconography in an entirely literal-minded fashion, as if its former meanings still automatically applied and as if Napoleon's claim to the throne was undisputed. Gros, by contrast, enters whole-heartedly into the pragmatic, instrumentalist spirit of Napoleonic propaganda, combining as he does sacred and secular, religious and rational justifications for Bonaparte's rule in a single painting without regard for ideological coherence. These contradictions were inherent in the regime, which owed its existence to the Revolution but, by the time that *Jaffa* was painted, was moving steadily towards monarchy.

*Figure 9.7   Michelangelo,* The Last Judgement, *detail (one of the damned), 1536–41, Sistine Chapel, Vatican, Vatican City, Rome. Photo: Scala.*

These contradictions were also inherent in the Egyptian campaign, which supposedly served to extend the enlightened (that is, secular, rational and modern) values of the Revolution into new regions but, in practice, substituted imperial expansion for revolutionary goals (it was, in fact, the prelude to France's colonization of North Africa in the nineteenth century). Just as Gros's *Jaffa* introduces a religious dimension into an image that ostensibly promotes the virtues of rationality, so his sketch for *The Battle of Nazareth* compromises its apparently 'scientific' documentary approach by altering the topography to give prominence to Christian holy sites such as Mount Tabor (which appears on the left when it should really be on the right); in fact, Bonaparte named the battle to highlight the notion of a Christian victory against the infidel, even though it did not take place that close to Nazareth. Gros's sketch also presents a moral contrast between European civilization and Oriental barbarism, which owes at least as much to Christian tradition as to the Enlightenment; in the centre, a French soldier spares the life of a surrendering foe, while a Turk in the lower left prepares to cut off the head of a defenceless enemy, only to be stopped by a bullet. The Arab figures caring for the sick in *Jaffa* also conform to European stereotypes but in a different, less overtly denigratory, fashion; their calmness in the face of the horrors of the plague was attributed by one Salon critic to their typically Oriental fatalism and passivity. As such, they can be seen as willing collaborators in the French colonial campaign. The point is that while Gros's painting acknowledges something of the horrors that took place in Jaffa, it works to conceal not only Bonaparte's crimes there but also the coercive and violent nature of the entire enterprise.

## Napoleon Visiting the Field of the Battle of Eylau

While *Eylau* (like *Jaffa*) contributes to the personality cult of Napoleon, it also addresses the human suffering caused by war with even greater directness than the earlier painting in which, as we have seen, the plague theme functions as a kind of alibi. *Eylau*, which was exhibited in the Salon of 1808, is concerned with one of the most horrific battles of the Napoleonic period. Before we take a closer look at how Gros depicted Eylau, it is important to note that the requirements of propaganda usually required the editing out of any too explicit reference to the violence of warfare. Thus, for example, though the commission for *The Battle of Nazareth* was cancelled mainly because Napoleon did not figure in the composition, it probably also had something to do with the gory nature of the scene. Critics of the time expressed disquiet about military paintings that (like Gros's sketch) dwelled on the actual killing involved, and thereby made it difficult for them to sustain a comforting belief in the noble ambitions that supposedly underlay French campaigns. They were too committed to this belief to be able to be explicit about the nature of their anxiety in their criticism, but it is not at all difficult to read between the lines.

Consider, for example, Pierre Chaussard's response to another painting by Gros, *The Battle of Aboukir* (see Plate 9.16), which was exhibited at the Salon of 1806 and depicts a further episode from the Egyptian campaign. Chaussard praised the contrast that it offered between French 'calm' and 'superiority' and 'the brutal rage and stupid ferocity' of the Orientals. As such, it presented, in Chaussard's words, 'the triumph of enlightenment and civilization over shadows and barbarism' (quoted in Prendergast, 1997, p.97). However, he also criticized the way that, as he saw it, the overall order of the composition is disrupted by the chaos and carnage of the scene. Chaussard would clearly prefer to ignore the violence that underlay France's 'civilizing mission'. Other critics of the time were even more disturbed by the painting. It was specifically the collapsing bodies of the Turks and the bright colours (the red perhaps too reminiscent of blood) that troubled them. What makes this example especially significant is that *The Battle of Aboukir* was *not* an official propaganda painting, but had been commissioned by one of the most famous of Napoleon's generals, Murat, who had led the charge which secured victory for the French at Aboukir in July 1799. He occupies the centre of Gros's composition.

By contrast, the first group of works commissioned by Denon (in 1806) virtually excluded scenes of French soldiers actually engaged in combat, even though all but one had a military subject. *The Battle of Austerlitz* (see Plate 9.17) by Gérard, for example, which was exhibited to great acclaim in 1810, does not show the heat of battle, but rather the moment when news of the victory was brought to Napoleon. The other works commissioned by Denon typically showed either the prelude to battle or its aftermath, and glorified Napoleon not as a military commander but rather as an inspiring, compassionate and magnanimous leader. A case in point is *Bonaparte Pardoning the Rebels of Cairo* (see Plate 9.18) by Pierre-Narcisse Guérin (1774–1833), another painting of the Egyptian campaign, which was exhibited in 1808; as you will probably not be surprised to learn, this image of a forgiving conqueror glosses over the brutality with which the French repressed the uprising that took place in Cairo in 1798.[43] In general, Napoleonic propaganda painting depicts the emperor as a 'great man', in accordance with the humanitarian and pacific values of the Enlightenment; it insists that, far from his being an aggressor, his endless wars are all motivated by a desire to establish peace.

One further point to be made about Napoleonic propaganda painting before we take a closer look at *Eylau* is that it was very tightly controlled. In 1806, for example, the list of subjects was devised by Denon in consultation with Napoleon. The exact moment to be depicted was specified in several cases; as the above examples indicate, this could be crucial in ensuring that any too overt representation of violence was avoided. Artists were simply allocated the subject that they were to paint, and were also required to submit sketches of their proposed compositions to Denon for approval. All of the paintings were to be ready for the Salon of 1808, and any artist who did not finish in time was to be ineligible for further commissions. In fact, Gérard and Gros (who was also supposed to depict an episode relating to the battle of Austerlitz) both failed to meet the deadline, but only because they were required to produce other paintings for the regime in the intervening period. In Gros's case, the work in question was *Napoleon Visiting the Field of the Battle of Eylau* (see Plate 9.19), the commission for which he was awarded in 1807 on winning a competition to commemorate the event.

The battle itself took place in Poland, near the village of Eylau, on 7–8 February 1807; the enemy force consisted largely of Russians. It was fought in a howling snowstorm, and the outcome remained uncertain on the morning of the 9th. Napoleon contemplated retreat but, when the

[43] For Stendhal's account of this episode, see LN, pp.37–8.

Russians did so first, he declared victory even though the French had suffered immense losses. Their casualties may have numbered as many as 30,000, while the Russians' have been put at up to 25,000. In the 58th *Bulletin de la Grande Armée*, which was devoted to an account of the battle, however, Napoleon put the figures at 1,900 French killed and 5,700 wounded. The *Bulletin* was one of the principal propaganda vehicles of the regime, serving to bring reports from the front into French homes. Its role was celebrated in a painting of 1807 by Louis-Léopold Boilly (1761–1845), *Reading the 'Bulletin of the Grande Armée'* (see Plate 9.20), which shows an entire family caught up in a patriotic fervour; even the breast-feeding mother is fulfilling what Napoleon considered to be women's primary function, that of producing new soldiers for the empire. Note, too, the bust of Napoleon on the mantelpiece, a copy after one made by the Italian sculptor Antonio Canova (1757–1822) (see Plate 9.21); such copies made Napoleon's image widely known. Of course, Boilly's painting does not correspond to the scepticism that we know actually characterized popular attitudes to reports in the *Bulletin* (remember the phrase 'lying like a bulletin' – see Units 7–8, p.79).

It was in the face of this kind of scepticism and, more specifically, in the face of widespread rumours that French losses were far higher than was admitted in the *Bulletin* that the imperial propaganda machine launched a campaign to persuade the French people that Eylau had been a great victory. The 58th *Bulletin*, which was printed in the official newspaper, *Le Moniteur*, on 24 February 1807, was followed by further bulletins countering reports of catastrophic losses. Since knowledge of what had happened could not be entirely suppressed, the regime needed to manipulate public opinion, and for this purpose official propaganda was less effective than reports that seemed to emanate from objective sources. This is why Napoleon himself dictated an 'eyewitness' report of the battle by a German, which appeared in the French press. It was as part of this exercise in damage control that the painting competition was announced by Denon in a letter to the press on 2 April. The logic behind it was that, if Eylau was indeed the victory that the regime claimed it was, then it must be capable of pictorial representation like the battle of Austerlitz. However, the terms of the competition were extremely tight; not only did the announcement include an account of the subject, but the letter also informed artists that a sketch of the site was available for consultation in Denon's offices.

---

**EXERCISE**   Now read Denon's account of the subject (Anthology I, pp.124–5) and consider the following questions. In each case, take as your point of reference other Napoleonic propaganda paintings and, in particular, Gros's *Jaffa*.

1   When and where exactly does the scene take place, and how does this contribute to the propaganda function of the proposed picture?

2     To what extent are the horrific consequences of the battle acknowledged, and how is this done in such a way as to contribute to the propaganda function of the proposed picture?

3     How is Napoleon himself presented, and how does the scene invoke France's 'civilizing mission'?

---

**DISCUSSION**     1     The scene is set on the morning after the battle, following other Napoleonic propaganda painting in deflecting attention from the actual violence. Also, by insisting that the scene is set on the battlefield, the text emphasizes that the French remained in possession of the field after the battle and thus are technically without doubt the victors; the reference to the French army having bivouacked there overnight stresses this point. This emphasis on the battlefield thus serves, like the tricolour flag in *Jaffa*, as a reminder of France's military prowess while avoiding depicting it directly.

2     The text acknowledges the horrific consequences to a remarkable extent, even referring to 'this vast field of carnage'. It also notes such grisly details as the way that dead bodies are heaped on top of the dying. Although this is exceptional by the standards of Napoleonic propaganda painting, it nevertheless distracts attention from the French losses by referring only to 'dead, dying and wounded' Russians and to 'long lines of Russian corpses'. The reference to the emperor speaking to the wounded 'in their own language' also identifies them as Russian (as well as contributing to the propaganda function of the work by flatteringly suggesting that Napoleon could speak Russian). In this respect, the scene might have been less disturbing to a French viewer than *Jaffa*, which it resembles in dealing with a military setback, since there the sufferers were actually French.

3     Napoleon is presented as a noble and compassionate figure, offering consolation to the wounded and making sure that they receive proper care. The text refers to his 'benevolent orders' and calls him a 'great man'. France's 'civilizing mission' is invoked by reference to the Russians' expectation that they will be killed – in accordance with their own 'barbarous' values – and their surprise and gratitude at receiving such care. The emphasis on medical care – the text even refers to hospitals – is reminiscent of *Jaffa*. Also, as in the earlier work, Napoleon appears as a quasi-spiritual figure in the way that he seems 'to alleviate the horrors of death, and to spread a gentler light over this scene of carnage'. The injured Lithuanian's speech also seems to credit him with almost supernatural powers of healing.

---

The scene broadly accords with Napoleon's bulletins, which similarly focus on the Russian casualties and, in expressing sorrow at the horrors of the battlefield, imply that the blame lies with other leaders: the sight, he wrote, 'is made to inspire in princes the love of peace and the abhorrence of war' (quoted in Prendergast, 1997, p.163). The incident with the Lithuanian was apparently Denon's invention. In his letter announcing the competition, Denon justifies the choice of moment by claiming it was made on the grounds that all battles resemble each other. He also says that the commission could simply have been entrusted to the 'painter of the hospital of Jaffa', who has 'already so well depicted a subject of this kind', but that it was only fair to give all artists a chance to secure it (Anthology I, p.123). This comment not only acknowledges the resemblance in subject to Gros's earlier painting, but also serves to justify the staging of a competition (Denon would have preferred to give the commission directly to Gros). The regime had ceased to allocate commissions by this means, largely because it did not allow it to have sufficient control over the result. There was also the risk that the public might dispute the jury's choice of winner. On this occasion, it reverted to this democratic practice in order to involve as many people as possible in the commemoration of the 'victory' but maintained strict control, with the result that the 26 competition entries were all quite similar. The example shown in the Illustrations Book is by Charles Meynier (1768–1832) (see Plate 9.22), who was placed second in the competition after Gros.

---

**EXERCISE**  What are the principal ways in which Gros's painting differs from Meynier's sketch, and what effect do they make?

Note: the wounded Lithuanian is the figure with upraised arm on the far left; the figure in the green coat is Murat.

---

**DISCUSSION**  Both compositions show Napoleon on horseback in the centre, but while Meynier depicts him looking straight towards the wounded Lithuanian, in Gros's painting his eyes are turned upwards and his hand is raised much higher as if in a gesture of benediction so that the spiritual aspect is emphasized. Gros also adds a Russian soldier kneeling by Napoleon's horse and leaning forward to kiss his imperial eagle, suggesting (as in *Jaffa*) that contact with the emperor's body has a miraculous power. Another difference is the much greater prominence that Gros gives to Murat, on a rearing horse and sumptuously dressed; the contrast with this bold and assertive figure highlights Napoleon's saintly compassion and further distances him from responsibility for the horrors on view. In Meynier's composition, the dead and dying in the foreground are (somewhat grotesquely) naked, but they do not dominate the space as much as those depicted by Gros, which lie in a confused heap, snow-sprinkled and blood-spattered, right across the front of the picture; there is even a corpse lying virtually beneath Napoleon's horse. Gros's foreground figures are also more vigorous, especially the wounded soldier on the right who pulls away from the doctor trying to tend him with a horrified expression on his face. In sum, Gros goes to greater extremes than Meynier, both in his exaltation of Napoleon and in his depiction of the horrors of the battlefield.

---

Although the prominence of the foreground figures disconcerted the critics when *Eylau* was exhibited in 1808, this can hardly be the result of any personal disaffection with Napoleon. In fact, Gros was so thrilled when the emperor gave him the Legion of Honour at the Salon that he proposed to celebrate the moment in a painting (see Figure 9.8). For one thing, in his treatment of the foreground, he was only taking advantage of a freedom that he was explicitly granted by the terms of the competition. Denon's letter states: 'Everything that is movable in the foreground is left absolutely up to the painter' (Anthology I, p.124). In any case, all the entries included similar (if not so brutal) details. A police report on the exhibition of the sketches stated uncomprehendingly that 'the artists have accumulated every kind of mutilation, the various results of a vast butchery, as if they had to paint precisely a scene of horror and carnage, and make war abhorrent' (quoted in Prendergast, 1997, p.17). The reason that the regime positively encouraged artists to engage with such subject matter is related not simply to what happened at Eylau but, more generally, to the profound war-weariness of the French people by this date. A major indicator of this was a growing resistance to conscription; significantly, one critic described the cheerful mood of Boilly's *The Conscripts of 1807* (see Plate 9.23) as 'unnatural' (quoted in Boime, 1990, p.48).

If Gros's painting was to succeed as propaganda, it had on some level to address these concerns rather than glorifying Napoleon as an invincible leader (which would not convince anyone). The regime's concern to *appear* to be responding to public opinion, which no doubt also contributed to the decision to stage a competition, can again be attributed to Napoleon's problems of political legitimation and his need to justify his authority as deriving from the people. In *Eylau*, therefore, the suffering caused by war is acknowledged (though displaced on to the enemy's soldiers), but the admission is counterbalanced by the portrayal of Napoleon as a humane leader. In other paintings of the later empire, the exploration of the experience of ordinary soldiers is given free rein. A notable example is *The Wounded Cuirassier* (see Plate 9.24) by Théodore Géricault (1791–1824), which depicts a cavalryman retreating from battle and owes a considerable debt to the work of Gros. The latter undoubtedly did play an important role in the move towards a new and typically 'Romantic' concern with suffering and with subjective experience. The crucial point, however, is that the initiative for doing so came not from Gros himself but from the Napoleonic regime.

*Figure 9.8  Antoine-Jean Gros,* Napoleon Distributing the Cross of the Legion of Honour to Artists at the Time of his Visit to the Salon of 1808, *unfinished, oil on canvas, 350 x 640 cm, Châteaux de Versailles et de Trianon. Photo: © RMN.*

# 4   The Decennial Competition of 1810

Official support for painting was motivated not simply by propaganda concerns but also by the belief that artistic achievements were crucial indicators of a regime's greatness. Part of the logic behind the emphasis on military painting, therefore, was the assumption that feats of arms and works of art *both* testified to the glory of Napoleonic rule. Traditionally, however, the most prestigious art form was the classical history painting, exemplified by David's *Oath of the Horatii* (Plate 9.1). As noted in the introduction to this unit, the superior status of this type of painting rested both on its idealized forms and on its elevated subject matter. From the later eighteenth century, however, depictions of modern history were defended and promoted on the grounds that they were more accessible and more relevant to a contemporary audience. More specifically, the claim was that subjects from national history encouraged patriotism. During the Revolution, these tensions between the ancient and the modern intensified. On the one hand, classical idealism, which seemed to transcend the specificities of time and place, was felt to accord with its universalist ideals; on the other hand, the need to uphold loyalty to the revolutionary cause encouraged the depiction of its principal actors and events. These tendencies are combined in David's *Marat* (Plate 9.7), which is as much a history painting as a portrait. The painting of national history triumphed under Napoleon, as revolutionary idealism (and republicanism) gave way to a pragmatic concern with promoting loyalty to himself as France's leader.

These tensions came to a head in the Decennial Competition of 1810, which was intended to reward the major artistic achievements of the decade since Napoleon came to power. Prizes were offered for the best history painting and for the best painting 'representing a subject honourable to the national character' (Wrigley, 1993, p.338). There were also prizes for sculpture and architecture. The jury consisted of members of the National Institute, the official body that regulated scholarship and the arts. In the first category, the front-runners were David's *Intervention of the Sabine Women* (see Plate 9.25) and *Scene from a Deluge* (see Plate 9.26), by Anne-Louis Girodet-Trioson (1767–1824), another former David pupil. The fact that the decision went in favour of Girodet indicates how far taste had moved away from the formal perfection of the classical ideal. By contrast to David's *Sabines*, with its poised antique nudes and overall sense of harmony, Girodet's *Deluge* represented a new extreme of violence and suffering; the moment depicted is one of high tension, since the splitting branch warns us that the family are about to be hurled into the abyss. Although the nudity and generalized drapery are conventional enough, the scene is not based on a literary text, as history paintings were supposed to be. It is tempting to speculate that Girodet's vision of humanity at the mercy of vast forces beyond their control had a particular resonance at the time, given that the French people were themselves helplessly caught up in the workings of the Napoleonic war machine.

In the second category, it was widely expected that the prize would go to Gros's *Jaffa*, which can be seen to represent a fundamental challenge to the classical traditions of history painting. The heroic male nude who dominated Davidian painting is here transformed into a helpless plague victim; the central figure in Girodet's *Deluge* is similarly helpless, but the difference in this case is that Gros also offers a new kind of hero, the modern military officer, in his tight, bright uniform. A further point of contrast between these two types of figure is that, whereas the male nude is a supposedly universal figure, the military officer's uniform identifies him with the particular nation that he serves or, of course, leads. This opposition can be brought into focus by reference to Canova's huge sculpture, *Napoleon as Mars the Peacemaker* (see Plate 9.27), which had been begun in 1803 but only arrived in Paris in 1811. It flatteringly portrays Napoleon in the guise of the god of war turned peacemaker and, on the sculptor's insistence, heroically nude; Canova had rejected Napoleon's proposal that he be depicted in his uniform. The rationale was precisely that nudity best befitted the hero by making his glory timeless. Napoleon's refusal to let the statue go on display was no doubt because he feared that its 'too athletic' forms would present an unflattering contrast to his own short and increasingly stout figure (quoted in Johns, 1998, p.101). More fundamentally, in view of his original proposal, his response can be seen to reflect his resolutely modern, pragmatic outlook, which meant that he had little time for classical idealism as such.

In the event, the jury decided that the prize in the second category should go to David for his *Coronation* (see Plate 9.28), which had been exhibited, like *Eylau*, at the Salon of 1808. There it had excited considerable interest, as Boilly recorded in one of his scenes of contemporary Parisian life (see Plate 9.29). In general, attendance figures for the Salon were high during the Napoleonic era, indicating that the regime's propaganda painting owed its success to the way it combined the traditional ambitions of high art with the spectacular appeal of popular entertainment. David had been commissioned to commemorate the coronation in his capacity as First Painter to the Emperor, a title he had been awarded in 1804. The title was a reversion to traditional royal practice (the Bourbon kings had also had their 'first painters'), just as the coronation ceremony itself was based on Bourbon ceremonial. The resulting painting demonstrates just how far the classical tradition had been undermined by the demands of Napoleonic propaganda. In it, David wholly abandons the visual austerity and sculptural simplicity of his earlier work in order to capture the magnificence of the ceremony in a riot of colour and a mass of detail. The actual moment that it depicts is crucial with respect to the new emperor's problems of political legitimation. Napoleon had had the Pope brought from Rome to crown him, but in the event, presumably partly to placate republican opinion by avoiding too overt connotations of divine right, placed the crown on his own head, thereby demonstrating that his ultimate source of legitimation was himself and his deeds. David originally intended to paint this provocative, give-away gesture, but was discouraged from doing so and instead showed Napoleon crowning Josephine.

In the end, the whole Decennial Competition collapsed and no prizes were awarded. First, the minister of the interior and then Napoleon himself challenged the jury's decisions, declaring that the winners ought to be David's *Sabines* and Gros's *Jaffa*. This turn of events confirms that competitions were inherently problematic for the regime because they did not allow for the degree of control that it required. It also suggests that the authorities felt obliged to pay lip-service (if no more) to the traditions of history painting and the superiority of the classical ideal, as exemplified by the *Sabines*. Napoleon also wanted the top prize to go to David as the greatest painter of the day, just as he wanted the main sculpture prize to go to Canova as the greatest sculptor (he had not then seen *Napoleon as Mars*); the acknowledgement of their genius would, he thought, do honour to the greatness of his rule. It also seems likely that the *Coronation* was considered an insufficiently patriotic picture to merit the other prize, given that all the other short-listed entries in the category focused on Napoleon's military exploits. *Jaffa* could be seen to be a truly national subject, dealing as it did with the achievements and suffering of the French people as represented by their army. By contrast, David's painting was primarily a dynastic picture, focusing as it did on the monarch, his wife and family. Part of the reason, in fact, that crowds gathered around it at the Salon was no doubt that the ceremony itself had been closed to the public. In the competition, as in Napoleonic propaganda painting generally, the regime's problems of legitimation made it politically necessary to balance ruler against people and, in however token a way, to represent them and their concerns as well as to glorify him.

# 5   Conclusion

The great advantage of history painting as a form of propaganda was that it could appear to be nothing of the kind. Whereas an official portrait of Napoleon fairly obviously served to focus loyalty towards the nation's leader, a depiction of a battle could be seen, on the one hand, as a work of art in its own right and, on the other, as an objective record of a historical event. This meant that the viewers whose attention was attracted by such a picture would be likely to absorb the version of reality that it presented without being aware of being manipulated. As we have seen, Napoleonic 'reality' involved extensive editing, both in terms of the selection of a particular moment and of the personages and actions to be included. A further example of this process is David's *Distribution of the Eagle Standards* (see Plate 9.30), exhibited at the Salon of 1810, which shows Napoleon accepting the army's oath of allegiance after his coronation; it was to have included Josephine seated on a throne behind Napoleon, but she had to be edited out after their divorce. In fact, this is widely considered to be one of David's weakest works. Part of the problem is that he had planned to depict a winged Victory flying over the heads of the soldiers and showering them with laurel leaves, but Napoleon compelled him to remove this figure too, with the result that the upper right of the composition appears strangely empty. The painting was poorly received by the critics, who found the balletic postures of the officers holding the eagle standards awkward and absurd. It succeeded neither as propaganda nor as a work of art.

Such interest and appeal as Napoleonic propaganda painting continues to have today depend on the extent to which it can be seen to transcend its original propaganda purpose – though, as we saw with Gros, this need not mean that it betrayed that purpose. The same might be said of another Napoleonic painting, Girodet's *Revolt at Cairo* (see Plate 9.31), also exhibited in 1810, the idea for which came from Napoleon himself and caused Denon some anxiety; he wrote that he wished the emperor had specified which moment of the revolt should be depicted. The subject – of insurgents resisting Napoleonic rule during the ill-fated Egyptian campaign – was disturbing and potentially subversive. Girodet's painting shows hand-to-hand combat in front of Cairo's main mosque; the composition sets a charging French hussar against a naked Arab warrior, who supports with one arm the collapsing body of a Mameluke.[44] Mamelukes were renowned for being brave, fierce, proud and beautiful, for their lavish costume and their taste for sodomy; as such, they epitomized both the degradation and the fascination of the East for Europeans. The painting could be read as an endorsement of colonialism, glossing over the brutal repression of the revolt and opposing French bravery and dignity to 'Oriental' cruelty and vice. Alternatively, it could be argued that the Arab and the Mameluke together constitute the main positive element of the composition, providing visual appeal and emotional interest. It is hard to pin down the significance of this violent and exotic spectacle either way, as promoting or subverting Napoleonic rule, as presenting Orientals as objects of disdain or desire. What does seem clear is that Girodet (who was probably homosexual and had royalist sympathies) brought his own personal agenda to the commission.

As we saw in the introduction with reference to Delacroix's *Massacres at Chios*, a concern with humble and anonymous figures, an interest in the exotic and the present-day and a fascination with violence and suffering are all characteristic of Romantic painting. In this respect, Girodet's painting represents a significant shift, despite retaining the hard-edged clarity and idealized nude bodies of Neoclassicism. More plausibly than with Gros, *The Revolt at Cairo* might be seen as embodying the artist's disaffection from the regime, his private concerns. Nevertheless, it remains the case that we are dealing here with official art, which allowed only to a limited extent for the expression of the concern with subjective experience that is fundamental to Romanticism. Equally, it is important to register that it would have been risky for an artist to give a critical edge to an officially commissioned work, given the highly repressive nature of the regime. This would have been especially true of paintings depicting Napoleon himself, such as *Jaffa* and *Eylau* or David's *Eagle Standards*, which has also been claimed to reveal the artist's disillusionment with Napoleon. According to the art historian who made this rather unlikely claim, David 'used the deletions he was forced to make as an opportunity to render the composition even more politically and aesthetically subversive' (Johnson, 1993, p.214). It is really only in English caricatures that we find a negative image of Napoleon (see Figure 9.5, p.122). Even after the fall of the empire, French representations are invariably positive, though now they showed him as a tragic hero, suffering in exile on St Helena, as well as continuing to promote the legend of the great leader who combined military genius with fellow-feeling for the common man.

[44] Originating as Circassian slaves (from the Caucasus), the Mamelukes were a military order who dominated Egypt between the early thirteenth and nineteenth centuries.

# References

Boime, A. (1990) *Art in an Age of Bonapartism*, Chicago, University of Chicago Press.

Brookner, A. (1980) *Jacques-Louis David*, London, Chatto and Windus.

Delacroix, E. (1938) *The Journal of Eugène Delacroix*, trans. Walter Pach, London, Jonathan Cape.

Delécluze, É.-J. (1983) *Louis David: Son école et son temps*, ed. J.-P. Mouilleseaux, Paris, Macola (first published 1855).

Grigsby, D.G. (1995) 'Rumor, contagion, and colonization in Gros's *Plague-Stricken of Jaffa*', *Representations*, 51, Summer, pp.1–46.

Johns, C.M. (1998) *Antonio Canova and the Politics of Patronage in Revolutionary and Napoleonic Europe*, Berkeley, University of California Press.

Johnson, D. (1993) *Jacques-Louis David: Art and Metamorphosis*, Princeton, Princeton University Press.

O'Brien, D. (1995) 'Antoine-Jean Gros in Italy', *Burlington Magazine*, 137, October, pp.651–60.

Porterfield, T. (1998) *The Allure of Empire: Art in the Service of French Imperialism 1798–1836*, Princeton, Princeton University Press.

Prendergast, C. (1997) *Napoleon and History Painting: Antoine-Jean Gros's 'La Bataille d'Eylau'*, Oxford, Oxford University Press.

Shelton, A.C. (1999) 'The critical reception of Ingres's portraits (1822–1855)', in G. Tinterow and P. Conisbee (eds) *Portraits by Ingres: Image of an Epoch*, New York, The Metropolitan Museum, pp.496–521.

Siegfried, S. (1980) 'The politics of criticism at the Salon of 1806: Ingres's *Napoleon Enthroned*', *Proceedings of the Consortium on Revolutionary Europe 1750–1850*, vol.2, pp.69–81.

Wrigley, R. (1993) *The Origins of French Art Criticism from the Ancien Régime to the Restoration*, Oxford, Oxford University Press.

# Further reading

Grigsby, D.G. (2002) *Extremities: Painting Empire in Post-Revolutionary France*, New Haven and London, Yale University Press.

Jourdan, A. (1998) *Napoléon: Héros, imperator, mécène*, Paris, Aubier.

O'Brien, D. (2003) 'Propaganda and the republic of the arts in Antoine-Jean Gros's *Napoleon visiting the Battlefield of Eylau the Morning after the Battle*', *French Historical Studies*, vol.26, no.2.

# Conclusion to Block 2

*Prepared for the course team by Emma Barker and Antony Lentin*

Curiosity about Napoleon remains compulsive. A Napoleon exhibition in Paris in 2002 listed 350 current books on him and 170 Internet sites. The main problem in coming to grips with Napoleon remains the spell, the enduring charisma, what Stendhal calls 'the magic of his being' (LN, p.115). For contemporaries, what he was, what he accomplished, what happened to him and what he left behind seemed too much, too awesome and on too vast a scale for mere mortals to grasp. 'The Napoleonic phenomenon' was perhaps the supreme example of what was known in the period as 'the sublime', something that took your breath away and suspended your critical judgement. In a characteristic Romantic reaction, the writer Chateaubriand (1768–1848), who broke with Napoleon after the murder of the Duke d'Enghien, deploring his dictatorial rule, nonetheless described him as 'a poet in action' and 'the mightiest breath of life which ever animated human clay' (quoted in Herold, 1955, p.xxxiv; Holtman, 1967, p.212).

No thinking person between 1800 and 1815 could ignore Napoleon, since the life of all Europe was affected by him directly or indirectly during those tumultuous years. The lives of both Stendhal and Staël were directly affected. Napoleon was aware that he did not ultimately win over the leading French writers of his day, though the next, younger generation of Romantics (including Stendhal), for whom he became an icon, soon made up for that. Chateaubriand and Staël, though as fascinated by him as Goethe was, soon came to mistrust and oppose him. Even Stendhal, while claiming that 'this man's whole life is a paean in praise of greatness of soul' (p.43), is in his way profoundly ambiguous about Napoleon. The Napoleonic epoch ended after all with a huge question mark. France was reduced to its frontiers of 1789. A million French soldiers had died in Napoleon's wars. What was it all for? What did it all mean? Staël claimed that 'the only thing that he brought to France, the only thing he could bring – was misery' (Anthology I, p.121). In the long aftermath following 1815, the nostalgic triumph of the Napoleonic legend, Chateaubriand too recalled the human cost:

> It is the fashion of the day to glorify Bonaparte's victories. Gone are the sufferers, and the victims' curses, their cries of pain, their howls of anguish are heard no more. Exhausted France no longer offers the spectacle of women ploughing the soil. No more are parents imprisoned as hostages for their sons, nor a whole village punished for the desertion of a conscript ... It is forgotten that everyone used to lament those victories, forgotten that the people, the court, the generals, the intimates of Napoleon were all weary of his oppression and his conquests, that they had had enough of a game which, when won, had to be played all over

again, enough of that existence which, because there was
nowhere to stop, was put to the hazard each morning.

(Quoted in Herold, 1987, pp.452–3)

These aspects of Napoleon's rule are barely mentioned by Stendhal. We
might add Napoleon's belief in reprisals when his will was flouted,
measures designed to deter and terrify, from the 'whiff of grapeshot' with
which he dispersed a royalist demonstration in 1795 to his ready resort to
the firing squad, from the political murder of the Duke d'Enghien to the
shooting of the patriotic German bookseller Johannes Palm (both
discussed by Stendhal). Napoleon had learned a certain ruthlessness from
the Jacobin Terror, though he came to detest and to victimize the
Jacobins. Even the *lettre de cachet* came back in the form of detention
without trial for political suspects and the administrative exile of Mme de
Staël. Yet in the years of his glory he undoubtedly enjoyed the
enthusiastic support of the new property owners in France whom he
protected from the threat of the *sans-culottes*, on the one hand, and the
émigré proprietors of the Old Regime, on the other. He won the
admiration of many beyond France, like Goethe and Byron. Above all he
retained the devotion of the rank-and-file through thick and thin.

Apart from the army, his main supporters during the Hundred Days
following his return from Elba in 1815 were the ordinary people whom
he inwardly despised and for whom he had done little. After his final
exile on St Helena and his death in 1821, absence made the heart grow
fonder, and attachment to his memory was further enhanced by the 15
years of reaction that followed Waterloo. In his well-known poem 'Le
Souvenir du peuple' ('Memories of the common people', 1827), Pierre
Jean de Béranger celebrated this popular veneration:

> On parlera de sa gloire
> Sous le chaume bien longtemps.

> [Folk will tell of his glory
> Beneath the thatch, for many a year to come.]

(Lucas, 1931, p.248; trans. Lentin)

# References

Herold, J.C. (ed.) (1955) *The Mind of Napoleon: A Selection from his
Written and Spoken Words*, New York, Columbia University Press.

Herold, J.C. (1987) *The Age of Napoleon*, New York, Houghton Mifflin.

Holtman, R.B. (1967) *The Napoleonic Revolution*, Philadelphia, J.B.
Lippincott.

Lucas, St J. (ed.) (1931) *The Oxford Book of French Verse*, Oxford,
Clarendon Press.

# Glossary

## Units 7–8

**Bas-relief** (also called low relief): sculpture in which the projection from the surface is very slight.

**Charter**: liberal French constitution granted by King Louis XVIII (r.1814–24) in 1814.

**Code Napoléon** (also known as the Civil Code): code of civil laws promulgated by Napoleon, 1804, and applied across the continental French empire.

**Concordat**: agreement between Napoleon and Pope Pius VII, promulgated in 1802, recognizing Catholicism as the majority religion in France in return for papal recognition of Napoleon's control of state and church.

**Congress of Vienna**: international conference held at Vienna in 1814–15 to determine the post-Napoleonic settlement of Europe.

**Great Powers**: Britain, Austria, Prussia and Russia.

**Holy Alliance**: agreement between the Great Powers, chiefly Russia and Austria, to maintain 'legitimacy' and suppress liberal movements in post-Napoleonic Europe.

**Primary source**: first-hand contemporary evidence attesting to a historical fact or event.

**Secondary source**: second-hand historical account, based on primary sources.

***Ultras*** (short for 'ultra-royalists'): reactionary supporters of the Bourbons under Louis XVIII, especially in the Chamber of Deputies.

**White Terror**: violent campaign of reprisals by Bourbon supporters against Bonapartists after the fall of Napoleon.

## Unit 9 (and block introduction)

**Form (noun)/formal (adjective)**: the term 'form' incorporates many aspects of the physical appearance and visual effects of painting and sculpture. They include perspective, depth, viewpoint (including angle of view), composition, colour, tone (light and shade), scale and proportion. The form of a work of art works with other factors – content and social, historical and psychological factors – to affect our interpretation of its meaning.

**Genre of painting**: see **hierarchy of the genres**.

**History painting**: the depiction of human life in its most exalted manifestations. Serious artists were expected to depict saints, heroes and so on, drawing their subjects from the Bible and ancient literature. See also **hierarchy of the genres**.

**Hierarchy of the genres** (in descending order):

1   history (including religious, historical, literary or mythological narratives, sometimes of an allegorical nature)

2   portraiture (the higher the status of the sitter, the higher that of the portrait)

3   genre (in the sense of scenes from everyday life)

4   landscape

5   still life.

**Iconography**: the study of the meanings of images. In art history the term is generally used to designate an approach that seeks to decode meaning through an attention to symbolism, etc. However, it can involve a consideration of formal features as well as subject matter. As applied to portraiture, it traditionally meant a list or catalogue of all the images of a particular person.

**Neoclassicism**: the term applied to late-eighteenth and early-nineteenth century painting in the classical style. Such painting forms part of an existing tradition of classicizing painting which can be traced back to the Renaissance, but is distinguished from it by (among other things) a greater concern with archaeological correctness in the imitation of antique forms.

**Painterly**: the opposite of linear style (a reliance on drawn, painted or sculpted lines for the principal effect in a work of art). A painterly approach relies on indeterminate patches of colour and/or looser brushwork for its principal effect, and creates a work in which areas are divided internally by 'soft' rather than 'hard' edges or contours.

**Salon**: the public exhibition held at the Louvre every year or two during the eighteenth and early nineteenth centuries; it took its name from the room in which it was held, the *salon carré* in the Louvre.

# Index